Stress Man:

Fast Proven ⌐
For Stress & Anxiety.

CW00859451

Sarah Wright

Table Of Contents

Let's End Stress In Our Lives Forever

"Happiness is a choice. You can choose to be happy. There's going to be stress in your life, but it's your choice whether you let it affect you or not."
Valeria Bertinelli

Stress is a feature in virtually everyone's life. It's something we all experience. But startlingly, very few of us actually know what to do about it. And more importantly, most of us don't know how to use it to our advantage. You don't have to have a high-pressure job, seven children, or an unusually fast paced life in order to experience stress. In fact, most other species in the animal kingdom also experience stress and I think it's safe to say that most of them aren't the head of multi-million dollar corporations! Of course, not all of us feel stress to the same degree. Depending on your personality and lifestyle, stress may come and go throughout your life, or it may be a constant feature.

It's hard to visualize what stress looks like because it varies so much between individuals. While some of us may be classic *"stress heads"*, banging around the house and shouting at the top of our lungs, a great deal more of us experience stress a lot more quietly. We stomach it, push it as far down as possible so it doesn't disturb our productivity or cause us to lash out at the people we love. But although this coping mechanism may seem to help when you're facing a crowd, it's not exactly addressing the problem. Ignoring stress doesn't make it go away, it only puts it off until tomorrow. Plus, having stress brewing in your gut can cause health problems, exhaustion, insomnia, relationship difficulties…the list goes on and on.

Think of stress like a bed and blanket. Imagine your life and all of its components as the bed. Let's say that you have children, a demanding mother-in-law, some people at work who aren't easy to be around, a credit card that you can't seem to pay off, and a busy schedule that's hard to keep up with. Think of those things as the bed of stress in your life. Now think about the ways your stress affects you. Think about your ability to focus and make decisions, think about your headaches and stomach upsets, think about how your thoughts race, how you always seem to be tired, and how short-tempered you can be. Imagine these effects as a blanket. With both a bed and a blanket of stress, it makes sense that so many of us feel like we're being crushed between two very uncomfortable forces when stress is high. If you've ever had insomnia you know that you can spend all night rearranging the covers, tossing and turning on a bed that feels like rocky ground, and still never get the peaceful rest your body requires. So if you imagine that your waking life is an extension of that - a sort of daytime insomnia - and that your waking *"bed and blankets"* are made entirely of stress, you can see how hard it can be to find the peace and tranquility you need to be your best self.

Stress holds us back in life. It clouds our thinking, making it hard to make effective decisions. It can even alter our personalities; making us lash out at work or snap at the people we love. On a physical level, stress can eat us from the inside out. Upset stomachs, headaches, sore shoulders and backs, insomnia, weight gain and weight loss, are the least of our problems if stress is allowed to take over our lives. Because high blood pressure, heart problems, strokes, peptic ulcers, and a world of other potential long-term illnesses can also develop as a result of stress and lifestyle alone.

Stress happens to everyone, and I cannot *stress* this enough. It happens when we face conflict, no matter how great or how small. It happens when our schedules are busy, when our car breaks down, when our family members are ill, when we have a lot of responsibilities to keep up with, when our finances are worrying, when we're working towards something important, when we're moving house or even planning a vacation. Stress is with us as we raise our children, from birth right through to their adult lives. It latches onto us when we're in periods of transition; when we're having a baby, when we get a new job or lose an old one, and when we experience shifts in our relationships. Stress is not a niche thing; it's a **human** thing. And if you want to live a happier, more productive and peaceful life, it's time to learn how to cope with it and use it as fuel for your success.

Take a moment to think about what your life would be like without stress. Visualize what life would be like if the people around you also eradicated stress from their lives.

Can you imagine the way we might speak to one another?
Can you picture yourself smiling because you actually feel like it, as opposed to smiling because that's what you to do to mask your stress?
Can you imagine having no tension in your neck and shoulders? Sleeping easily at night?
Feeling like you have more time and energy to devote to your family and doing the things you love?
Can you imagine sailing through hard times because you're better equipped to deal with them?
Can you imagine achieving serenity?

"Sometimes when people are under stress, they hate to think, and it's the time when they most need to think."
William J. Clinton

The aim of this book is to make all the things you just imagined, a **reality**. Life is for living. It's for happiness and enjoyment. In this fast paced world, we often forget about the importance of our own peace and joy. We get so caught up with the things we *have* to do that we don't make time to do the things we *want* to do. We work so much that we're too exhausted to do anything else. At home with our children, we focus on homework, laundry, school runs and packed lunches. We forget to actually spend quality time with our families because we're so focused on the mundanities of daily life. We don't take day trips as much as we'd like. We wish we had more time and energy to meet up with our friends and blow off steam. And many times this is because even when we do spend quality time with the people we love, our minds are elsewhere. There never seems to be enough hours in a day. We're preoccupied with whatever it is that's causing us stress rather than being able to fully commit to the moments we're in. It's hard to be fully present, when your mind is locked in past failures and future worries. But no matter who you are, it is possible to prioritize happiness and enjoyment of life. We just have to learn how to manage our stress levels and strike a work / rest balance. We have to know what to *do* with our stress in order to make it work for us, not against us.

As human beings, we have an immense ability to grow and change. We can learn new things, apply them to our lives, and become better versions of ourselves for as long as we live. It's an incredible part of our existence and something we should celebrate. When we dedicate ourselves to becoming more *emotionally intelligent*, we will naturally be better equipped to understand our response to stress triggers. We will understand our feelings and behaviors on a deeper level. Therefore, we can reform and reshape the ways we cope with stress. We can change the way we live in order to make things easier on ourselves. We can learn to prioritize more effectively. We can have the life we really want. We are each in control of our own destiny. You are in control of yours, and I'm in control of mine. Let yourself be empowered by that. You've made the decision to do something about your stress, and now you're ready to get into action.

Think of today as the beginning of a new chapter. Take some time now to think about what you want to get out of this book. Visualize yourself the way you'd like your life to be. Imagine your stress getting smaller and smaller. Picture it receding into the background of your life until it is only a dot in the distance. This book is going to guide you through how to achieve just that. Together, we're going to find the positive attributes of your stress - the things that you can actually use to your advantage - and hold them close to your chest. But the rest of your stress - the harmful and frustrating parts of it - we will diminish and push as far away from you as possible. Let's get started!

Your New Life

"You may have a fresh start any moment you choose, for this thing we call 'failure' is not the falling down, but the staying down."
Mary Pickford

Before moving on to the methods for diminishing stress, take ten minutes or so to write down at least five things you would like to get out of this book. You might want to feel stronger in the face of conflict or get a better quality of sleep each night. You might want to learn how to truly relax or how to have fun despite the serious stuff in life. You might want to lessen your stress or learn how to deal with it better. Or maybe you'd like to be more productive and lessen the amount of worry and anxiety you experience. For now, don't let yourself worry about *how* you're going to get these things. There is nothing you can gain by worrying about stress…apart from more stress. Just write down where you'd like to be at the end of this journey. When you're finished, pin your list somewhere that you'll be able to see it every day.

Take time to read your list at least once a day. This could be done either first thing in the morning, last thing at night, or both. Give yourself a moment to really visualize yourself reaching those goals every time you do this. Your goals are achievable, so try to think of them as beacons of hope rather than allowing yourself to be cynical or skeptical of them. Life is yours for the taking, so make sure you believe in yourself and that truth. Make a pledge to yourself now. Promise yourself that you will do everything in your power to get the peace you need and deserve.

Take a brief moment now to rate your stress levels as they are today from 1 to 10, with 1 being cool as a cucumber and 10 being red hot. This is something I will encourage you to do throughout your journey, as it is a simple way to keep track of your progress. You may also want to write down any specific things that you feel are contributing to your stress and how your stress is affecting you. If you're not a big fan of journaling, do not worry, just keep it simple.

Remember, you're not getting graded on this. You're doing it for yourself so that you can get hold of and conquer your stress.

Plotting your progress is a great way to find out which stress busters work for you and which ones don't. Remember that we are all individuals and there is no single book or technique that will work for everyone. So it's important that you take a proactive role in your journey to serenity. This book has been developed in a way that there should plenty of helpful tools for everyone, but don't worry if one or two things don't work for you. That is absolutely normal. Just know that, although I will provide you with plenty of guidance, you are the one in the driver's seat. You will get as much out of this as you put in, so try to care enough about yourself to really get stuck in.

The 7-Day Start-Up Plan – It's Time For A Reboot!

"Planning is bringing the future into the present so that you can do something about it now."
Alan Lakein

It's not easy to make a lot big life changes all at once. But we all know that when we read a book like this, we want answers as quickly as possible. We want immediate results. This book is going to guide you through a plethora of long-term changes, but this first section is designed to give you the short-term changes you crave, so that you can get a positive kick-start to your new stress-free life. Stress management involves a lot of skills and a certain mindset. It takes practice and patience. But rather than having you get to the end of this book before you see any results, I'm encouraging you to get into action today. Because if you bought this book, you need things to start changing today. However, in saying that, if you prefer to skip the start-up plan and get straight into the deeper sections of this book, it will do you no harm to do so. This is your journey, and you should always do what's right for you.

The *7 day start-up plan* will give you guidelines on how to get structure and order into your days, but it will also place a good deal of importance on rest, recreation, quiet time and exercise. These are things that we all must learn to prioritize and implement into our every day life if we're going to successfully beat stress. It's very possible that the start-up plan may be a challenge, especially if you're used to spending your days focusing on work and other people. But if you follow the program you will reap a ton of benefits such as learning how to prioritize yourself and your needs, getting used to being quiet and still, and socializing with others in positive ways to balance out the negative things in life. You may also find that your sleep patterns improve and that you have more physical and mental energy that will help you get more things done throughout your days. You will also likely notice that your mind will gradually become clearer because you will be giving it plenty of time to recuperate. Finally, the 7-day start-up plan will provide you with a strong foundation that will serve you well as you work through the rest of the stress management guidelines in this book.

Before you get started, there are a few things you should do to prepare so that you get the most out of your start-up plan. So, before getting started, take a decent amount of time to do the following preparations:

1- Start by writing a meal plan for the next 7 days.
Doing this ahead of time will free your mind up for more important decisions. It will give you less to think about over the course of the week so that you can have more time and energy to focus on the important things in your life. You can narrow this down to 7 dinners if you're not keen on planning breakfasts and lunches, but if you want to be really prepared, include all your meals on this list. This is all about making things as easy on you as possible so try not to skip this preparation.

2 - Next, write down a few types of exercise that you enjoy.
If the gym is not your thing, think outside the box. Other ways you can get exercise into your life might include shopping, yoga, hiking, having sex, taking a walk along the beach with a friend, dancing, playing in the back yard with your kids, playing sports, etc. For the purpose of the start-up plan, keep this simple. You will have plenty of time to add on more exercise and self-improvements as time goes

on so go easy on yourself for now. Just write down a few things that you enjoy that will get your body moving. Endorphins play a big part in stress management so this is important. Having this list on hand will make it easier to decide what types of exercise you can fit in on any given day. Again, it's about making decisions as easy as possible. Be careful not to overwhelm yourself by forcing yourself to go to the gym everyday or trying to change too much at once. Ease yourself in.

3 - Schedule in a minimum of one relaxing treatment this week.
This could be getting a massage, attending a meditation class, getting acupuncture, enjoying a spa day, anything that's going to make you feel relaxed and refreshed. Book this in advance so that it's not on your to do list during the 7 day start-up. This way you'll be less likely to cancel if you're too busy. Learning to prioritize your need for self-care, rest, and relaxation is an extremely important part of stress management. So commit yourself to making time for these things from the start. We need to send ourselves messages of self-love and self-care. We need to do things that are solely for the purpose of enjoyment and peace.

4 - Next, write a list of quiet activities that you enjoy.
Do not include anything that involves screens on this list. Instead, think of things like reading, taking a bath, gardening, painting, stargazing, bird watching, baking, going to the museum or art galleries, taking a walk without your mobile phone, etc. Again, having this list ahead of time means that when it's time for quiet time in your start-up week, you won't have to expend too much brain power thinking about what to do. Don't forget that these should be things you *enjoy*. There is no point of putting things on your list if you don't actually like doing them! So consider writing things down that you haven't been able to fit in lately, things you wish you could do more often, things that make you feel relaxed, and things that are purely for your own enjoyment. This is not a time to multi-task. So if you don't like baking, don't class baking your friend's birthday cake as quiet time for that day. If you don't like weeding out the garden, don't cheat yourself by calling that quiet time. Make sure that you get enjoyable quiet time in addition to things you *have* to do.

5 - Before you get started, you're also going to want to decide on a bedtime.

Sleep deprivation and not having enough structure in your days are some of the worst things for stress levels. Going to bed at the same time every night will get your body and mind on more stable ground. It will help recharge your batteries so that your mind and your mood are clear and calm. So think about how much sleep you need to function at your best and set your bedtime accordingly. Think of this as getting your body clock reset and normalized. There are apps available on most mobile phones that will tell you when to go to bed and when to wake. So if you think this is something that you're likely to struggle with, something like this may be of help. Similarly, if you have a partner and your routines are closely linked, you will need to have their support in order to make these changes. That might mean that you both do it together or it might mean that you'll have to have separate bedtime routines. Talk about it and do what works for you.

6 - Finally, decide on a diary keeping method that will work well for you.

This shouldn't be something to stress out about so don't put too much pressure on yourself. It should just be an easy way to keep track of your progress. Some people will want to recap how they felt all through the day; they might like to write long entries about everything that happened. Other people might find it easier to simply rate their stress levels from 1-10 at the end of each day and jot down a few notes on the most important things that happened. What's important is that you suit yourself. The one thing I would advise when it comes to journaling is to be careful about writing down too much negativity. Journaling your negative emotions can be helpful, especially if you're not comfortable talking about your feelings or you need help understanding them. However, when you're journaling try your best to keep things on a positive tip or to balance any negativity with some positivity. Your journal should not be a place to rant and complain, as this is likely to wind you up and may be unproductive. Keep this in mind especially if you journal before going to bed as you don't want to become emotionally activated when you need a good restful sleep.

Now that you've done all the preparations, the only thing left to think about is when to begin your start-up plan. As we all have different lives and different schedules, this will be different for everyone, but I'd encourage you to start on a non-work day to make things as easy as possible. If you work Monday to Friday, start your plan on Saturday or Sunday. Similarly, it might be best to look ahead at what's in store for you each day of the start-up plan so that you can aptly prepare for anything that might impede on your normal schedule.

Lastly, in order to keep you on track with your daily tasks without overwhelming yourself, use care when writing out to do lists. If you have a long running to do list, this might be contributing to your stress. So, I'd advise that you keep that list for your reference but instead of working off that list all the time, write smaller, more achievable to do lists for each day. Transfer anything from your big list to your daily lists *only* if you can achieve them that day. Having smaller lists each day protects you from being overwhelmed while giving you an opportunity to actually finish everything on your list. This is a great way to keep yourself motivated while giving you the chance to feel a sense of accomplishment. I will mention this again throughout this book and I highly recommend that you take it on board. Any small change that can make a big difference is always worth trying.

Getting Started With Your New Life

Day One

"With the new day comes new strength and new thoughts."
Eleanor Roosevelt.

Begin each day the same way. Start by eating a healthy breakfast, then write a to do list for the day. Writing a list of daily tasks first thing in the morning means that you won't have to think about them again until it's time to do them. Try not to put too much on your to do list and do not put anything on the list that can or should be done on another day. Day one is all about easing yourself in, so go about your day as you usually would. Make sure to eat well by not skipping meals or eating a lot of salty or sugary snacks. Try to keep caffeine, alcohol, and any other substances to a minimum. Remember that you're trying to reset your body systems. So giving them a break from any harmful or toxic substances that could alter your sleep patterns or dull your alertness is going to be of great benefit.

On day one you will need to take at least 30 minutes of *"me time"* and a further 30 consecutive minutes of screen-free time. Your *"me time"* can be spent doing anything on your lists of quiet activities or exercise. Although *"me time"* should generally be time spent alone, if you don't get enough time to be with your children, partner or friends due to a busy schedule, use this time to hang out with them. However, during this time make a rule that none of you should talk about work, school, or things that need to be done. Use this time to play a game together, read together, or talk about other things. Often families get so caught up in the daily comings and goings of life that they forget to enjoy each other's company. It's important that we take the time to do this.

Your 30 consecutive minutes of screen-free time should be spent away from computers, tablets, video games, and mobile phones. If 30 minutes is easy for you, make it an hour or more. The point is to give your eyes and brain more time to recover than you normally would. During this time, do something from your list of quiet activities or take the time to simply sit outside or in a dark room and be still. Do not listen to music or a podcast. If you find it hard to separate yourself from your phone, put it in another room or give it to a family member or friend until your 30 minutes are up. As you progress through this plan and the book in general, you will be encouraged to spend increasing amounts of time away from screens so that your brain and eyes can rest and recuperate. There can be a lot of stress wrapped up in our screens, so making a point to separate yourself from them is a means of protecting yourself and regaining your autonomy.

At the end of day one, start a new and improved bedtime routine. Our bodies and minds depend on structure to be at their best so try to go to sleep at the same time every night and do the same routine each night. Read a magazine for a half hour, give yourself a facial, have a shave or whatever you feel you need to do to get into sleep mode. Try to stay off screens for at least 30 minutes before you go to sleep and avoid having the TV on in your bedroom while you sleep. Your brain doesn't want to be stimulated while you rest, so give it the break it deserves. Day one is over.

Day Two

"Every day is a new day, and you'll never be able to find happiness if you don't move on."
Carrie Underwood

Begin the day by eating a healthy breakfast and writing out your to do list. Day two will build on what you did yesterday. You will need to take 30 minutes of quiet time, where you can do anything on your list of quiet activities or simply sit and be still. In addition to this, you will need to take another 30-60 consecutive minutes of screen-free time. As always, if this is too easy for you, feel free to take more. Resist the temptation to use your 30 minutes of quiet time as your screen-free time. The aim is to increase the amount of time your brain has to rest and recover, *not* to multitask your quiet time!

You will have two extra tasks to do today. The first will be to eat three meals without multitasking. Don't listen to your headphones or make phone calls. Don't scroll through social media or do your Internet shopping. Just sit and eat. Focus on your food and let your mind breathe. Focus on chewing. Think about how your food tastes and feels in your mouth. This is a practice in being present and mindful. It is one that, once you become good at it, will be of great use in other parts of life. Being able to be *present* could mean that you'll be able to swim where you'd otherwise sink.

The second task you're going to do is to think of something you could get help with and ask for it. This is an important challenge for people who regularly do everything themselves. When we're stressed out it can be really hard to reach out and ask for help. But being able to ask for help is a skill and it's one to be treasured. So think about things at work and at home and ask yourself if there's anything you could get help with. Perhaps there's a task at work that you'd value a second opinion on. Perhaps you'll ask your partner to do the grocery shopping for the week. Maybe you'll need to ask a friend for their expertise on something you've been struggling with. Maybe you need to move a large piece of furniture and you need help lifting it. Whatever it is, it is the active asking for help that's important. We need to train our minds into knowing that asking for help does not mean failure. It doesn't mean that you can't do something for yourself. It simply means that you are confident and secure enough in yourself to use your resources wisely. It's learning how to manage tasks more efficiently so as to ensure less stress.

Remember to eat well on day two. Reduce the amount of unhealthy snacks you consume and increase the amount of good stuff on your plate. At nighttime, follow the bedtime routine that you set for yourself on day one and remember to stay away from screens for at least 30 minutes before bed.

Day Three

"Every new beginning comes from some other beginning's end."
Seneca

Start with a healthy breakfast and write out your to do list as usual. Today is going to build on what you've done on the previous two days while adding some time for personal reflection.

Today you should aim get 1 to 1.5 consecutive hours of screen-free time. Try to schedule this time into your daily comings and goings so that you don't have a reason to get out of doing it. Pick a time of day when you're not expecting any important phone calls or emails. Your screen-free time does not have to be quiet time unless you want it to be. You can spend it exercising, relaxing, or enjoying time with friends and family. The important thing is to get a sense of feeling grounded and calm. It's a time to make room for face-to-face communication, laughter, and enjoyment, or to simply spend some time feeling at peace.

In addition to your screen-free time today, take a 30 to 60 minute walk without wearing headphones or making phone calls. Walking is a good form of exercise, which will help you produce some happy brain chemicals, increase your energy levels, and help you get a better night's sleep. But more importantly, use this time to think and decompress. Think about things in your life and how they make you feel. Allow yourself to feel your emotions and listen to your thoughts. In the hustle and bustle of daily life, we often miss out on the time we need to process our feelings. The more we keep these things at the back of our mind, the more likely we are to experience an increase in stress, insomnia, and mood disturbances. If we don't allow ourselves time to process, we might get into more arguments with the people we love. We might be more easily wound up or feel constantly agitated. Also, when you think while your body is moving, you get the sensation that you are actively, *physically* working through things. If you find that you have quite a lot on your mind or that the things you're thinking about are upsetting you, that is absolutely fine. Your negative thoughts need to be heard. Your feelings need to be felt. However, if that is the case, give yourself an extra 5-10 minutes to think positively before returning home or going back to the office. Leave your negative energy out on the street and feel good about giving yourself the time to work through it.

Lastly on day three, challenge yourself to delegate at least one task to someone else. This might mean telling the kids to clean up their toys or pack their own lunch rather than doing it for them. It might mean having a colleague make a phone call for you. The best way to delegate is to look at your to do list and ask yourself if everything on the list really must be done by *you*. If you're snowed under, being able to delegate less important tasks can reduce the amount of pressure you're under. Resist the urge to believe that you're the only person who can do anything right. Things of less importance will be fine in someone else's hands.

Tonight as usual, finish the day with your chosen bedtime routine. Remember to rate your stress from 1-10 and to keep your thoughts in a positive place so that you can rest peacefully through the night. Try to maintain a screen-free bedtime as well.

Day Four

"In three words I can sum up everything I've learned about life: it goes on."
Robert Frost

Begin your day as you have on the previous three days. Remember to keep your breakfast healthy and keep your to do list as succinct as possible. If something can be done on another day, keep it off today's list.

Today, you should spend 1 to 1.5 consecutive hours of screen-free time. You can do more than this if you like. Use this time however you choose but do try to do something enjoyable if at all possible. The aim is to create habits of good self care and bring more light into your daily life. Too much screen time can put up walls between ourselves and the people we love. It can also create unrest and impatience of the mind and body. Using your screen-free time to lighten up and have fun will leave you feeling refreshed and energized. Perhaps today you could use your screen-free time to play a game of cards or kick a ball around with your friends or your kids. Maybe you'll use it to play an instrument or try out a new recipe. Maybe you'll use it as quiet time or time to take a walk with the dog.

If at all possible, try not to use your screen-free time to work, as the focus should be on prioritizing your enjoyment of life. This is vital for stress management.

For today's extra challenge, do something meditative such as painting, coloring, baking, formally meditating or listening to quiet music in a dimly lit room. You could sit somewhere peaceful and watch the clouds go by or get your hands in the dirt by doing some gardening or going to the beach. You might want to do yoga or listen to a guided relaxation online. This meditative activity should last around an hour or more. If you have trouble finding the time for this, think outside the box and make it a priority. Maybe you could wake up an hour earlier or use your lunch break. Maybe you'll need to give up some TV time or spend less time browsing social media. Whatever you have to do, remember that it's for the best. Prioritize your need for calm.

You are now over halfway through your start-up plan. As you wind down into your bedtime routine, think about how you're feeling. Do you feel any benefits yet? Are there certain things you've enjoyed and others you haven't? Remember that it's important to know and do what's right for you during your journey. Reflecting on how things are going as you progress will help you develop a better understanding of yourself and your needs. Take some time to write down one or two things that you've gotten out of the last few days. Have you learned anything about yourself? Rate your stress from 1-10 and commence bedtime as usual.

Day Five

"Don't dwell on what went wrong. Instead, focus on what to do next. Spend your energies on moving forward toward finding the answer."
Denis Waitley

Wake up and start your day as usual. Remind yourself of the importance of a healthy diet as you prepare your breakfast. Remind yourself of the importance of simplicity as you write your to do list. After breakfast, take five minutes to breathe deeply and quietly before moving on with your day. Harness positivity and serenity. Repel negativity and worry.

Today you should aim to take 1.5 to 2 consecutive hours of screen-free time. Remember to schedule this at a time when you are not expecting any important calls or emails so as not to be interrupted. Spend this time alone or with loved ones. Spend it relaxing or exercising. If you're not sure what you'd like to do with your screen-free time, refer to the lists you wrote before you embarked on your start-up week. That's what they're there for.

You will have two added challenges today. The first is to get some extra exercise, so pick one or two things from your exercise list and get busy! Your second added challenge for today is to contact someone you've been meaning to get in touch with but haven't had the time to recently. This could be an old friend, an extended family member, someone you've been meaning to congratulate or console. Taking the time to be social and be around the people we love is extremely important when it comes to feeling good about ourselves and the world around us. It helps us prioritize communication and togetherness. This is something that often gets lost in our lives in this day and age. Once you have reached out, schedule a date to hang out. Meet up for coffee, take a walk together, go out to a concert, have a meal together, or if your schedules are hard to work with, schedule in a phone call so that you can properly catch up. When our schedules are busy, life can become monotonous. There are fewer times to be excited, and fewer times to feel good. So it's important that we maintain our relationships with people that have a positive effect on us. It's important that we do things outside our normal daily routine.

End your night the way you have all week. Again, before you go to sleep take some time to reflect on how you're feeling. Rate your stress levels from 1-10 and if you feel inclined to do so, write down some things you're feeling good about. Remember that positive thinking takes practice so doing exercises like this is really important when building a positive foundation for a stress free life. Plus, going to bed with positive thoughts in your mind will promote a more restful sleep and an easier wake up in the morning.

Day Six

"Don't brood. Get on with living and loving. You don't have forever."
Leo Buscaglia.

You are nearly at the end of your start-up and you should already feel like you've got more control over your moods and your life in general. You will hopefully be enjoying the time you're taking to relax, unwind, and have fun. At this stage, your routine should be starting to set in, so as usual, wake, eat a healthy breakfast, and write out your to do list.

Today you should aim to have at least 2 consecutive hours of screen-free time. You can of course, make this longer if you like. If you were particularly tied to your screens before this endeavor, you may be starting to feel liberated when you're away from them now. If that isn't the case yet, just stick with it. It will get easier and more enjoyable as you go along. Today, use your screen-free time however you choose. Be productive or do some relaxation. Prepare a big dinner for yourself or take a nap. Whatever feels right for you.

In addition to your screen-free time, you should also get 30 to 60 minutes of recreation today. Ideally, this time should be spent with friends or family but if you have a solo hobby that you'd prefer to work on, go for it! The aim is to have fun and get energized. Time like this is obviously great for your mood and your social life, but it can also help release tension and ensure a better night's sleep.

For your added challenge today, think about any unfinished projects that are hanging over you. These could be things in work or things at home. You may be helping a friend complete a home renovation or you may be halfway through an art project. Unfinished business could be any number of things and most of us have at least one of these things hanging onto the bottom of our long running to do lists! Once you've identified the task, make time in your schedule to get it done no later than next week. Or, if you have time today, why not tackle it now? Unfinished projects can add a silent weight to our minds. We might not always be aware of them, but they're always there. Freeing yourself from this weight will obviously make you feel lighter as well as giving you a sense of accomplishment. This is a good way to get motivated and to feel proud of yourself. We need to get these good feelings wherever we can.

Remember to keep eating well and keep alcohol and caffeine to a minimum. Before bed tonight, take some time to reflect. What, if any, changes can you identify in your life so far?

Are you sleeping better?
Eating better?
Getting more done?
Smiling more?
Thinking about things that don't include work or other stressful forces?
Enjoying your time with others more?
Do you feel like you have more control over your life yet?

Write down a few positive things and rate your stress from 1-10 as usual.

Day Seven

"The journey of a thousand miles begins with one step."
Lao Tzu

Congratulations on reaching the final day of your start-up plan! If you've been following the plan, you should feel different in some way today. You might feel as though you're learning something. You may feel more positive. You may simply be intrigued and ready to get into the next step of your journey. You may have learned that certain things worked well for you and others didn't. This is powerful knowledge to have on your side. Because the more you know about yourself and your habits, the better equipped you will be to combat stress.

Today you should start your day as you have been all week. Remember that when you are eating breakfast, you should avoid multitasking. Just concentrate on eating. Write out your to do list for the day and remember to keep it succinct and achievable. Set yourself up for a win!

Again, today you should aim for at least 2 consecutive hours of screen-free time and a further 30 to 60 minutes of quiet time. Look at your list of relaxing activities and choose one or two to indulge in. Bring a book into the bath with you. Sit outside and listen to the birds. Do some stretching or a guided meditation.

Your added challenge for day seven is to go somewhere that you haven't been in a while. This should be somewhere you like, such as a taking a long drive to get out of the city, visiting a local beach, taking a hike through the woods, eating at a favorite restaurant, or visiting your hometown. When life is busy, we often let things like this fall by the wayside. We don't take the time to do things and go places for the sheer purpose of enjoyment. We're often too tired after a long day or week at work. We often feel like we have too much to do. But doing things like this is a great way to get some head space and harness positivity. It's a good way to get in the habit of taking good care of yourself inside and out.

Tonight, as you wind down for bedtime, remember to reflect. Think about what things were like before the 7-day start-up plan and think about how things will be afterwards. Have your daily 1-10 ratings illustrated any change yet? Will you continue to designate screen-free time each day? Will you remember to have fun? Will you try to connect more with the people you love? Have you benefited from quiet time? Do you find it easier to defuse now?

This plan has been designed almost like a stress management boot camp. It has given you some guidance on how to better structure your days and how to prioritize yourself and your needs amidst the stressful forces in your life. The rest of this book will take a much deeper look into long-term stress management. It will take you through things you can do to prevent stress every day as well as how to cope when you're in the height of a stressful moment. There will be more focus placed on managing your online life as well as some in-depth looks at specific stress-related issues such as relationship difficulties and how to simplify complicated lives. As you read on, try to keep your routine as close to how it was during the start-up plan as possible. Structure should be a lifelong facet of your life. Yes, structure is great to implement in a crisis, but it's even better at preventing a crisis, so make sure that you do prioritize your body and mind's need for it along your journey.

Keeping Stress At Bay, Every Day

"Its not stress that kills us, it is our reaction to it."
Hans Selye

Stress is a complex and wide ranging issue. Each one of us has our own lifestyle and our own obstacles, so it is only natural that we will each experience stress in a variety of ways to varying degrees. However, regardless of what your home and work life are like, there are things all of us can do every day to prevent stress and make coping with it easier. This section will provide you with a vast number of things you can do every day to alleviate the impact stress has on you. It is my firm belief that we should not only focus on getting rid of stress, but more importantly, that we should prevent it from getting into our heads in the first place. We must do everything we can day in and day out to ensure a peaceful and positive outlook on life; because every moment of serenity we achieve has the power to lessen the degree to which stress affects us. Refer to the following list as often as necessary and do your best to turn these preventative measures into habits in your daily life. The more you practice good self-care on a daily basis, the stronger you will be when times are tough. Your self-esteem will benefit and your tolerance for difficulties will increase. So try not to breeze through this section too quickly.

Everyday Rules For a Stress Free Life

1 - Take care of number one.

"If people concentrated on the really important things in life, there would be a shortage of fishing poles."
Doug Larson

It is incredibly easy and common for people to put themselves last on their priority list. If you have a spouse or partner, children, friendships to maintain, difficulties in your extended family, a demanding career or any other number of responsibilities in your life, it is very possible that you may end up putting yourself last on the list of things that need taken care of. But we all know deep down that if you don't take care of yourself, you won't be very good at taking care of anyone or anything else. Think of this like a safety talk on an airplane. When the oxygen masks drop down, we are always told to put our mask on before helping another person, including our children. Now, I am not suggesting that you take your kids off your priority list, but if you don't take measures to ensure that you are strong and properly equipped to deal with your own problems, how can you expect to be any good for anyone else? If you allow yourself to become rundown or you stretch yourself too thin, it is likely that you will eventually reach a point of melt down.

It is immensely important that we strike a work / play balance. These days, most of us work long hours. We take on a lot of projects at once, our kids are involved in more extracurricular activities than we ever were, and our social lives are a source of near constant demand due to the fact that mobile phones and social media have made us contactable at all times. In this day and age, we are becoming less and less likely to prioritize taking good care of ourselves amidst the plethora of responsibilities we are all juggling.

But what happens when we're all work and no play? Put simply: **Stress.** When we don't take care of ourselves, eventually things are going to come to a head. Our work will suffer. We will get into fights with the people we're close to. We'll feel like we're constantly working against the clock. We'll fill every minute of every day with things we have to do. But when will we do the things we *want* to do? When we will be brave enough to schedule in some much needed *"me time"*? We have to be able to prioritize more effectively. Because letting yourself become run down will only make coping with stress more difficult.

If you want to be more productive and have more energy to give to others at work and at home, you've got to prevent your systems from becoming depleted. Believe it or not, when it comes to stress and productivity, those who take sufficient recreational time for themselves will be more able to reach their goals and exceed their own expectations. Therefore, it is imperative that you schedule in some time each week that is purely for relaxation and recreation.

We have to remember that life is for living. By scheduling in some *"play time"* a few times each week, you are giving your body and mind time to break free of the things that are holding you down. You are letting yourself blow off steam, and you are giving yourself a chance to lighten up. Human beings have a fundamental need for play. That means that taking time to have fun should be considered a mandatory feature in your life. So whatever it is that you like to do, whether you enjoy taking baths, playing sports, going out with friends, or reading a good book, remind yourself throughout each week that these things are just as important as the rest of the things on your to do list. Do not let a week go by without enjoyment and relaxation.

What to do:
Take a few minutes to write a list of ten things that you enjoy doing just for the sake of it. If you did the 7-Day Start Up, you should already have some of these written up. Put your list somewhere where you will see it every day. Make it a rule that you must do at least three things on your list each week. Doing this is fundamentally important when it comes to keeping stress at bay, so don't give yourself a choice in the matter. If you think you'll find it hard to prioritize things like this, schedule them into your diary or set reminders on your phone. Look into your daily comings and goings and see if there is any time that you can steal for yourself. Use your lunch breaks to sit outdoors with a book or take a walk through a park. Wake up an hour earlier than usual or change the way you approach the weekend so that you can get an extra hour to yourself here and there. The world can be really hard on us, so it's extremely important that we be good to ourselves.

2 - Place due focus on your physical health.

"If you treat every situation as a life and death matter, you'll die a lot of times."
Dean Smith

It should come as no major shock to know that if your physical health is in the toilet, your mental health is probably soon to follow. If we eat a lot of salty, sugary, fatty foods, and don't get the nutrients our body requires, we are obviously more likely to become run down. And what happens when we get run down? Our stress levels rise because we're not in the right position to deal with all the things on our metaphorical plate. So too, if we don't get enough exercise, we are not only doing ourselves physical harm, but we are also starving ourselves of one of the greatest outlets for relieving stress.

Exercising - be it working hard at the gym or simply getting out on long walks with the dog - helps the body relieve tension and provides us with substantial endorphins and serotonin to help us maintain a stable mood and a positive mental attitude. Taking on an exercise program is also great for getting in some necessary *"me time"* as well as providing yourself with challenges. Overcoming physical challenges is a fantastic way to increase your self-esteem and your motivation in other parts of life. And guess what else, for those of you who struggle with insomnia, exercise presents an opportunity for you to tire yourself out. Getting plenty of exercise should never be underestimated when it comes to your health and the way you approach obstacles in other parts of life. On top of all the other benefits, exercise can also present an opportunity to work through things in your head and put your frustrations into a physical forum; a place where you can burn through those things while you're burning calories.

In order to be especially good to your body, we all know that we have to eat properly. However, there is a problem that arises for many of us when we think about "taking care" of our health. I'm talking about the overwhelming pressure to lose weight. If we go on a diet for the wrong reasons, we might end up doing ourselves more harm than good. Yes, it is extremely important to keep your weight under control for your physical health and your self-image; however, the way we go about losing weight is where many of us are led astray. For many people, "dieting" actually means starving their body of vital nutrients. And although you may temporarily look better, you might not be giving your body all it needs to run smoothly. So, just as it is important not to overload your body with unhealthy foods, it's also important to make sure that you're giving yourself all the nutrients you need to maintain your personal lifestyle.

Remember that we are all different and our diets should reflect that. If you work out a lot, you'll need extra protein. If you experience low blood sugar, you may feel tired, get repetitive bouts of headaches and nausea, feel dizzy or lightheaded, and find it hard to focus, or make poor decisions. That could mean that you'll be better off eating little and often. If your life is very demanding on the mind, you'll need to increase the amount of *"brain foods"* you consume. You get the gist. The focus on your physical health is the most important thing here. If you're not getting all the things your body needs, you may become short tempered or experience a period of low mood. And of course, if you're not taking care of your immune system, you could very easily come down with recurrent colds and flus. If you're someone who gets cold sores, you'll know that when you're not taking care of yourself and your stress levels are high, you're likely to see one (or more) surface. The moral of the story is, stress and physical health are very closely linked. Take some time to think about how you normally eat and drink, and what your lifestyle requires of you. Think about your sleep patterns and your drinking habits. Be honest with yourself and try to identify any ways that you can better take care of yourself.

The thing to remember here is balance and moderation. Don't skip meals and don't eat too much junk food. Don't starve yourself and don't binge eat. Don't drink too much alcohol. Monitor how much caffeine you're taking in each day. Get plenty of sleep. Stop smoking. These are not ground breaking ideas; you should already know all of this. But if you want to be able to better manage your stress, you've got to give your body the right fuel. Do not underestimate the power of good physical health.

What to do:
Take a minute or two to think about anything you may be starving your body of.

Do you get enough exercise?

Do you eat plenty of nutrient rich foods?
Do you drink plenty of water?

Now think about anything you're doing to your body that you think might need to change.

Do you eat too much junk food?
Do you eat at irregular times?
Do you drink too much alcohol or smoke?

Write down one or two things that you'd like to change in the next few weeks. Resist the urge to write down too many things at the start. This is not an excuse to swamp yourself with even more things on your to do list, or to be hard on yourself. Trying to change too much at once rarely works out, so take it easy. There's no need to stress yourself out about it! Tackling one or two things is plenty for now. You can always add more to your list later.

Implementing a change in your routine can be a bit jarring; however, after three or four weeks, your body and mind will naturally settle into the changes you've made. Generally speaking, it takes roughly 21 to 28 days to create a new habit, so make sure you stick with it long enough for that habit to gain some strength. After that, you can think about adding another change or two into your health plan. As you move towards a healthier lifestyle, take time to recognize any positive effects you feel. Do you have more energy? Do you feel like you are more focused? Are you sleeping better? Taking time for self-reflection is really important when you're working on self-improvement. Focusing on positive changes gives you an opportunity to pat yourself on the back and stay motivated. It's important to be able to recognize your hard work and prevent yourself from becoming bored.

3 - Take time to be quiet.

"Rest is not idleness, and to lie sometimes on the grass under the trees on a summer's day, listening to the murmur of water, or watching the clouds float across the sky, is by no means a waste of time."

John Lubbock

It's hard to express just how important it is to get quiet time in our lives. But we can start by simply thinking about what life was like before the Internet. Before we had mobile phones and social media, our lives were a lot more private. We spent our free time meeting up with friends, reading books, and getting outdoors. Life was quieter back then. We worked shorter hours and spent more time with our families. We had time alone. Time without being contactable, time to think, and time to relax. Unfortunately, we can't go backwards in time and most of us could never live without our mobile phone and Wi-Fi. But our necessity for quiet time hasn't changed just because our way of life has.

Nowadays, many of us are surrounded by noise throughout our days. When we commute to and from work, we've got headphones on. When we do housework, we listen to podcasts or have the TV on in the background. We spend our time in waiting rooms scrolling through pictures and updates posted by people we haven't even seen in person for months or even years. Now that we are contactable at all times, work doesn't stop when we leave the office. Our friends and family text all day and night. We're running around like headless chickens most of the time and the background of this way of life, is *noise*.

Without taking sufficient quiet time, we can start to feel antagonized, frazzled, aggravated, frustrated, and exhausted. The thing is, we've become so used to the noise that silencing it can feel a little disorienting. If you're used to living a fast paced life, the idea of sitting down and being quiet might actually sound a little hellish, because how will you possibly be able to relax when you have so much to do? But in time you will see that the more quiet time you take, the more you will benefit from it. Well-rested minds make the best decisions. A quiet brain can cope better with conflict, mistakes, and setbacks. We need to be able to hear our own thoughts and think clearly. Once your brain is allowed to cut through all the noise in life, your stress levels will drop like lead.

So what exactly is quiet time and how can we get some? Start by setting boundaries with your mobile phone. People will contact you all day every day if you let them, whether it's business or personal. But as you probably know, this can cause anxiety and disruption to your daily life. So you've got to set some rules. You might want to set a cut off time for texts and calls, especially for business purposes. If you work a nine to five job, perhaps you should only respond to work related messages from 8AM to 6PM. For personal texts, maybe you should stop texting a few hours before bedtime so that you have a chance to wind down and focus on yourself. Challenge yourself to leave your phone at home while you walk the dog or run your errands. You'll be the one setting these rules here, so make sure they're going to be practical and fit into your life.

Next, put a limit on emails. We shouldn't feel pressured to have to respond to every email right away, so putting in some structure and boundaries into your emailing practices could really help to alleviate that pressure. Consider only answering emails at set times, twice or three times each day. Let's say that you check your emails first thing in the morning, mid afternoon, and just before dinnertime, unless there is something that really can't wait. If you receive an email that isn't urgent, it can wait until your designated email times. Once your mobile and email boundaries are in place, limit your TV time and the amount of time you spend on social media. Set a timer for these things and keep a strong resolve about it. You have to give your eyes a break and your mind a chance to breathe.

One of the best things we can do for ourselves is to secure some screen-free time every day. Again, if you followed the 7-day start-up plan, you'll be familiar with this idea by this point. Breaking the tie between you and your electronic devices can be extremely liberating. This might mean keeping your weekends free of technology or simply taking an hour or two away from screens each evening.

Staring at screens for too long creates unrest in our minds and bodies. We're becoming too used to being constantly stimulated. Apart from the strain on our eyes and the headaches we get from too much screen time, we need to be able to exist quietly and mindfully if we're ever going to conquer stress. Screens can make us extremely impatient. We need to allow our own thoughts to come and go without feeling bombarded by other people's thoughts. We need to remember how to entertain ourselves away from screens, to be able to think creatively again. We need to remember to look around us and see the beauty in the world. Time spent like this brings you back down to earth. It reminds you of the simple things in the world and can help to clarify what it is that really makes you happy. And as an added benefit, it's a lot easier to find a solution to our problems when we give ourselves the gift of peace and quiet.

What to do:
This week, count up the amount of time you spend away from screens. This includes phones, computers, tablets and TVs.

Do you take any time away from these things?
How would you feel if you left your phone at home for the day? Be honest!
How often do you take time to just sit quietly and let yourself think?
Is your life lacking quiet time?
Is your mind constantly "buzzing"?

If so, it's probably time to give it a break! Once you know how much time you usually spend away from screens, aim to double it. If you spend two hours away from screens this week, make it four next week. If you don't spend any time away from screens, start with two hours each week. This should be attainable no matter who you are or what your life is like. Two hours is roughly four dinners. It's two relaxing baths. It's a walk along the beach. It's a couple of chapters in that book you've been wanting to read. You can achieve two hours. Ideally, you should aim to be away from screens for an hour or two per day at the very least. Ditch your phone at your lunch break. Close your laptop and sit in your backyard or a local park for half an hour. Look out the window of a bus and take in the what's happening in the world around you, rather than staring at a social media feed when traveling to and from work. These are subtle changes that can make a huge impact on your stress levels.

Finally, once you've mastered *quiet time*, challenge yourself to try out *silent time*. Silent time is about turning everything off, inside and out. It's about sitting and simply being present. You might want to try out meditation to help train your mind to be quiet, but if that's not for you, just challenge yourself to stop *doing* all the time. Take quiet time a step further by sitting silently and doing nothing for 30 to 60 minutes, as opposed to doing the dishes quietly or paying your bills quietly. Let your thoughts drift from one thing to another. Resist the urge to dwell on conflict or to create a to do list in your mind. Thoughts will come and go and that's fine. Don't fight them or worry about them. Just listen to your thoughts, acknowledge them, and let them pass. Give yourself a break from it all. You deserve that much.

4 - Resist procrastination at all costs.

"Nothing is so fatiguing as the eternal hanging on of an uncompleted task."
William James

We all know that procrastination can act like a wrecking ball to virtually any project we're working on. It holds us back from completing tasks. It steals our attention when we're trying to get things done. It leads us into the arms of less important tasks, rather than allowing us to take care of the things we should be focusing on. And as I'm sure you know, when you fall behind in your schedule, or fail to complete things on time, your stress levels will naturally increase. Not completing tasks means having more things on your to do list and more pressure to get them done, not to mention potential feelings of failure and disappointment.

For some reason, when we procrastinate, we often turn away from the most important things on our to do list, accomplishing menial, consequence-free tasks instead. But every time we do this, the important things on our list seem to become bigger and more important, and therefore, daunting. The more we avoid something, the harder it is to face. So rather than putting your all into writing up a new CV, you'll rearrange your cupboards. Instead of organizing your paper work towards the end of the tax year, you'll waste your time sifting through that basket of unmatched socks. It's almost like when we do this, we're deliberately making things harder on ourselves. We're getting in our own way and setting ourselves up for failure and frustration.

Of course, procrastination can be a lot worse than that, because it doesn't always encourage us to deal with the smaller things on our lists. Many times, procrastination doesn't want us to accomplish anything. And we all know what that looks like. It's worth thinking about what your habits tell you about yourself, because where procrastination takes root, stress is sure to grow. So ask yourself a few questions to see if you can make sense of what's underneath your inclination to put things off until *later*.

Do you procrastinate because you're self sabotaging?
If so, why?
Are you afraid of failure?
Are you finding it hard to focus because there's just too much on your plate?
Are you afraid of taking risks?
Are you holding yourself back from progression in your career or your passion?
Are you just a daydreamer who finds it hard to knuckle down?

Understanding why you procrastinate can help you harness the tools you need to break through those tendencies and get on with your life. This, in turn, will help you get better at multitasking and stress management.

It's important to note that procrastination is extremely common. It can happen when we only have a couple of things on our to do list, but often it kicks into overdrive when we're overwhelmed with tasks and responsibilities. If you're facing a lot of big tasks, it's only natural to feel anxious. And it is in these times that so many of us bury our heads in the sand. Instead of chipping away at the things we have to do little by little, we're turning away from them in the hopes that they'll just magically go away. Instead of only getting a few things done, we end up getting nothing done.

But we all know that the things on our to do lists rarely go away on their own. We will have to turn back and get them done eventually.

And as you probably know, so many times when we do finally get stuck in, we realize that we've made a mountain out of a molehill. That thing that you've been putting off for weeks might only take a couple of hours in a single day to accomplish. Trying to ignore it for so long means that we've allowed it to become this huge, insurmountable, stressful thing in our heads. We've given it more importance than it originally needed. We've basically just freaked ourselves out over something we could've done with relative ease.

When it comes to procrastination, we have to have the nerve to face our to do lists head on, with confidence. We have to be able to take one thing at a time. So instead of looking at everything that needs done, we need to just focus on the thing we're doing right **now**. We need to forgive ourselves for procrastinating and prove to ourselves that we can overcome it. We also need to ask ourselves why we're procrastinating so we can nip it in the bud. In moments like these, it may be helpful to think about other times when you have overcome procrastination. Let the evidence of that time motivate you to get your head back in the game. You are totally capable of doing the things you want to accomplish.

What to do:
Think again, about how procrastination features in your life but this time, take that thought process one step further. This time, think about how procrastination is related to your stress. We are all individuals so this process will naturally be different for everyone. Try to identify any connections between the two. Does procrastination cause you stress? Does stress cause you to procrastinate? For some of us, having too much to do and too much to think about (a.k.a. stress) can make us throw our hands in the air and just give up (a.k.a. procrastination). This is a common response when times are particularly demanding. If you're juggling too many things, it's possible that instead of dropping one, you'll actually just drop them all. Unfortunately, most of the things we're juggling aren't optional. They are things we can't get out of, like taking care of our kids, keeping up with things at work, taking care of our health, nursing a sick pet, etc.

So how on earth can we keep up with everything without feeling stressed or procrastinating? Start by writing some lists. Break down the things you have to do into smaller, simpler tasks. For instance, if you're moving house, you're bound to have a to do list that seems endless. Breaking things down into smaller tasks might sound like a bad idea because it'll actually make your list longer, but smaller tasks are easier to manage and getting them done means you'll be crossing more things off your list. This is kind of a way to trick your mind into getting more done by changing your perspective. Being able to see things this way can take the panic out of larger tasks. So rather than writing "pack" on your moving house list, break packing down into a few different tasks, such as "pack books", "pack kitchen appliances", "pack winter clothes", etc.

Smaller, simpler tasks put less pressure on the mind and crossing things off your list is a great way to get the motivation and feelings of accomplishment you need to conquer the next task. Once you've broken your list down into more manageable tasks, break it down even further. Do this by writing lists for the next seven days with specific tasks designated for each day. For instance, "Monday: pack books, call lawyer, ask boss about time off, get kids to pack the toys they won't need until moving day", "Tuesday: pack winter clothes, call mom and dad, organize painters", etc.

By doing this, you are giving yourself one compact list to look at each day rather than getting a few things done on a huge list and not being able to sleep because there's still so much to do. Do your Monday list and then stop thinking about it. Don't let yourself worry about anything else that needs done this week. Tomorrow, do Tuesday's list and stop thinking about it once it's complete. This is a great way to manage tasks when it comes to procrastination and stress. The aim is to prevent yourself from becoming overwhelmed or worked up by the amount of tasks you have to do in the long run. Focus on today's list only.

Productive stress management is all about creating the illusion of a more manageable life. When stress has your thinking all jumbled up, this type of task management can take the flurry and worry away and put confidence and assurance in its place. Just remember that once you're done with today's list, you are not allowed to then start worrying about tomorrow's list. You've done what you have to do for the day and now it's time to focus on other things.

5 - Learn how to say, 'No'.

"Focusing is about saying no."
Steve Jobs

When it comes to lessening and preventing stress, there are very few lessons as important as getting comfortable with saying, 'no'. For those of us who tend to take on too many tasks at once, being able to say, 'no' will make a sizable difference where our stress levels are concerned. Sometimes it's more important to get some head space than it is to help an acquaintance move house or run the PTA bake sale. Sometimes we have to let ourselves finish what we're working on before taking on another project.

In order to reduce the number of things we have to do, we have to be able to rate the importance of tasks appropriately. For instance, if you have been offered extra work that's going to make you some much needed extra cash, you're going to want to say, 'yes'. But doing so might mean that you have to say, 'no' to other things, and that's okay. Sometimes we worry that by saying, 'no' to our friends and family when they need us, we're letting them down. We worry that if we don't offer to help out a friend in need, we're not being a good friend. We might think that if we say, 'no' to meeting up for coffee or a night out, people will think badly of us. But if your friends and family members have any respect for you, they will understand if you tell them that you're just too busy right now. You don't have to volunteer your time if you don't have any time to spare. You don't have to agree to do things that you have no energy for. We can't all do everything all the time. We have to be able to prioritize ourselves and take care of the things that matter most before we can take more on.

What to do:
Start by recognizing if you're the type of person that agrees to do more than you're actually capable of. It can feel really great to help

other people out, but if helping them out means stressing yourself out, that feeling is null and void. When someone asks you do something, take a breath before you blurt out 'yes'. Tell them that you need to think about it and then take some time to see if you can actually fit it into your schedule. This can give you the time and space you need to realistically assess the situation at hand and lessen the pressure to make a quick decision. Think about your schedule, your energy levels and your stress levels. Then ask yourself if this is something you can easily fit into your life right now or not. If you can, remember to also consider if it's going to be beneficial to you and your life. Why take something on if it's only going to cause you grief?

If you need to say, 'no', remember that you can always offer to pitch in later when things calm down a bit, or express that you're sorry you can't get involved this time around. You could also help by potentially offering advice on how someone can proceed without you. Maybe you could offer to do a little bit on said project rather than going all in. The real habit changer here is taking the time to realistically assess the situation without blindly agreeing to do something that's going to cause you added stress in the future. Finally, don't beat yourself up if you're not available for everyone you know, 24/7. You are only human and you have to take care of number one first.

6 - Stop insisting on doing everything yourself.

"Deciding what not to do is as important as deciding what to do."
Jessica Jackley

So many of us get stuck in the habit of doing absolutely everything by ourselves. The most common reason for this is that a lot of times it just seems easier to do everything rather than risking having someone else do things differently or poorly. But despite the fact that this is a very common habit, it can have disastrous effects on your mood and seriously ramp up your stress levels. Firstly, insisting on doing everything by yourself obviously adds an extra heap of tasks on your to do list. But there are consequences beyond that. When we insist on believing that we're the only person that can get the job done correctly, we're setting ourselves up for aggravation and frustration when other people simply do things differently than we would have. Avoiding situations like this could mean drastically lowering your stress levels.

One of the reasons people develop tendencies like this is that they need to feel like they are in control. By doing everything themselves, they know they can get the job done right. However, without gaining some perspective and being realistic about the importance of the task at hand, this could easily make every molehill into a mountain. You have to be able to ask yourself if the task at hand is important enough to insist on doing it yourself. You have to ask yourself if it's okay to have this particular job be done a little differently to how you would do it yourself. You have to ask yourself if there are more important things you could be spending your time and energy on.

Who cares if your partner doesn't know exactly how you pack the kids' lunches? I'm sure they can work it out.

Who cares if someone at work doesn't have the same telephone manner that you do? Are they going to sink the company over it?

Who cares if someone else has to figure out how to make doctor appointments or write notes to your children's teachers?

Or if someone has to look something up online when you already know the answer?

These are just examples, but you can see where I'm coming from. A lot of times, relinquishing control of menial or less important tasks means that you will have more mental and physical energy to sink into more important tasks. Why drive yourself crazy about the little things?

What to do:
When someone offers to help, just say, 'yes'. Yes, most of our daily tasks will be done differently if someone else takes over. But you have to ask yourself how important this thing really is. Is it worth stressing out about? Is it worth adding another thing on your to do

list? Is it possible that having someone else do things slightly differently won't really matter in the long run? That it could actually *help* to have something taken off your to do list?

Relinquishing control can be really hard to do, but you have to think of it in the broader scheme of things. Attempting to control everything rarely leads to a peaceful mind. So rather than insisting on doing everything yourself, delegate smaller tasks to other people at work and at home. Get some perspective, assess the importance of the task at hand, and relinquish control of the smaller things to other people. Going grocery shopping shouldn't be allowed to add stress to your life. Neither should laundry, telephone calls, basic family admin, getting the kids where they need to be each day, etc. If you're stressing out about things like this, address it by asking for help from the people around you. Save your energy for the big stuff in life rather than filling your plate with a buffet of stress-inducers.

7 - Master the art of time management.

"By failing to prepare, you are preparing to fail."
Benjamin Franklin

Being well organized has tons of benefits. Organization helps us get things done as easily and quickly as possible, and when it comes to stress, it's not hard to see that being better organized is always going to be a good thing. Managing your time effectively will undoubtedly lead to less stress all around. When we have a clear plan to follow, we're more likely to stay on track. So keeping a daily diary to tell you what to do with your time is essential. Diaries and reminders on your computer or mobile phone are fantastic tools when it comes to keeping things in order and getting stuff done. Many of us lead busy lives and there's a lot to keep track of. Why rely on your brain to remember everything you have to do and when you have to do it, when you could simply write it down? Remember to use a system that works for you.

Furthermore, in order to really manage your time well, you want to think in terms of *companion tasks*. By companion tasks, I don't mean things that necessarily go together, but rather they are things that can be achieved in the same time or place. Times when you can kill two birds with one stone. For instance, what can you do with the time you have between dropping your kid at cheerleading practice and picking them up? Is there a shop nearby that has something you need for work? Do you need to do some banking? Could you organize your weekly schedule while you wait in the car?

This isn't ground breaking thinking, most of us do as much as we can all the time, but bringing this type of thinking into other spheres of your life could be very beneficial. The aim is to kill as many metaphorical birds as possible with a single stone. So schedule your shopping trips in a way that will make it easy for you to get as many things at once. If the hardware store is next to the grocery store, get everything you need in one trip. If there is something you use a lot of such as laundry detergent, buy it in bulk so you can save time and money. In fact, if you purchase all of your long life grocery items in bulk, your trips to the grocery store will take less time and you'll save money. It's all about thinking how you can get more time out of your days. Planning meals ahead of each week is one great way of doing this. When you write a meal plan, you take into consideration what's happening on each day. So when you know you're going to be late coming home from work one day, you'll have something convenient on hand for when you get in. You can also save a ton of money if you do your grocery shopping after you plan your meals, so this is always going to be a good idea.

You may also want to consider waking up earlier or rearranging your schedule to make things easier on you. Basically, if you feel like you're always short of time, you'll probably benefit from sitting down and thinking about how you steal time for yourself. Think of your life objectively, like a problem solving case. If you were advising a friend, what tips might you offer them? Are there things you do that are a waste of your time? Could you work faster or smarter? Ultimately, the answer will have to come from within, but taking time to brainstorm and work through time management issues is always time well spent.

What to do:

Think about how your days and weeks are organized. Is there anything that you feel just isn't working? Are there tasks that you dread doing, such as laundry or shopping? If so, how could you change the structure of your days to make those things easier? Maybe it would be easier to drop your laundry off at a wash-dry-fold service rather than spending a few hours every week on it. Maybe you could buy in bulk to reduce the time and travel costs of shopping every week, or perhaps you could do your grocery shopping online? Could you possibly wake up an hour earlier and/or stay up an hour later in order to get more time out of your day? Is there anything you do that could be considered a waste of time?

With things like this, it's important to think outside the box. Also, do not underestimate the worth of trial and error. It doesn't hurt to try out new things and if they don't work out, move on and try something else. For now, write a list of tasks that you feel are draining you of your time and energy. However long or short your list is, getting things down on paper will help you to think of them objectively and logistically. Remember to take one thing at a time so as to not get worked up during this process. Talk to your partner or a friend about your unwelcome time-draining tasks and see if they might have some new ideas or any advice. With things like this, a lot of times just having another brain on board can be a big help.

Are there any things on your plate that you could ask someone else to do so that you can cross it off your list completely? Are there two or three tasks that you could do at the same time rather than spending more time doing them separately? Could you afford to get someone in to clean the house once in a while to free yourself up for more important things? Could you organize a few meetings on the same day in the same location to save you running around all week? For instance, maybe you'll have a business meeting at 10am in a coffee shop, an interview with a potential babysitter in the same place at 11am, and coffee with a few friends at 12pm. Being smart about where and when you schedule things could make things dramatically easier on you, while freeing up your time so that you can spend it doing the things you want to do.

8 - Challenge yourself.

"Being challenged in life is inevitable, being defeated is optional."
Roger Crawford

There are few things in life that have the power to motivate us the way overcoming challenges does. Overcoming challenges gives us a chance for self-growth. When we accomplish things that we're historically "bad" at, we immediately feel more competent and more confident. Being stressed out can really take a toll on you. It can make you feel like you're not good enough and it can make you want to give up on things that you really could accomplish if you weren't under so much stress. Life often feels like we're climbing a big steep mountain that has few rewards along the way. However, when we feel like we're slaying it - like we're giving it all we've got and we can be proud of ourselves - that mountain feels less daunting and the process is more enjoyable.

We know that stress can make us feel frazzled and unsure of ourselves. But we also know that when we overcome something we feel confident, proud, and capable. And those positive feelings can really drive us forward. They can give us the guts to keep pushing. They can give us the motivation we need for the next hurdle. So why not create some challenges for yourself that you know will lead to a sense of pride and accomplishment? A challenge can be absolutely anything. You might want to get into something fitness related or take a pottery class. You might want to lose a few pounds or sink more energy into a neglected hobby. Have you any unfinished projects around the house? Challenge yourself to finish them this week. Have you anything you've always wanted to be good at but never put the time into it? Do it now. Schedule it into your life and dedicate yourself to achieving it. The key is to harvest some of those good feelings. We need to feel good about ourselves and life in general so that we're less shaken when stress is high.

What to do:
Think about a challenge that you'd like to overcome. You don't have to climb Mount Everest or cure a disease. You could lose 5 pounds or spend a day baking challah bread. You could sign up for a dance class or read a thousand page novel. Why not ask a friend to join you

in a challenge so that you have someone to egg you on? Or create a family challenge in the house such as clearing out a spare room to make an office or a playroom for the kids?

You get the gist. The aim is to set yourself up for a win. So don't make things too hard on yourself and don't take on a challenge that you're more than likely to fail. Remember, this is just an exercise to get you pumped up and feeling positive about yourself and your life. And if you get a few things done in the meantime, all the better.

9 - Treat yourself with kindness.

"Until you value yourself, you won't value your time. Until you value your time, you will not do anything with it."
M. Scott Peck

When you're stressed out, the last thing you need is to beat yourself up or focus on your failures and shortcomings. Human beings have an immense capacity for self-loathing and self doubt; and on the battlefield of stress, those tendencies are going to leave you and your troops either beaten down or waving a white flag. When times are tough, we need to be able to be our own best friends, not our worst enemies. We need to know when it's time for tough love versus when it's just time for love. We have to be able to forgive ourselves when things don't go the way we planned. Because if all we do is beat ourselves up when things go wrong, how we will ever harness the confidence and willingness to give things another go?

Sometimes, in order to get perspective, you have to imagine yourself as though you were someone else. For instance, imagine it were a friend who dropped the ball in work. What would you say to that person? Would you tell them that they failed because they're not good enough? Would you tell them that they're terrible at their job and that they should just give up? Would you tell them there's no point even trying to redeem themselves? No, you wouldn't. You'd build them up, tell them to go easy on themselves, and give them a little love and motivation. So why is it that when it's us who have failed, we don't do that for ourselves? We get angry with ourselves and put ourselves down.

In life, there will be failures. There will be times when you don't live up to your personal best. There will be times when things just get on top of you and some of the things in your life will suffer for it. But that's okay. That's life. None of us are on it 100% of the time. We have to be able to get through our shortcomings by accepting and loving ourselves no matter what. Being overly harsh on yourself rarely leads to success. Being able to lift yourself up after a fall is a true virtue. Be gentle with yourself. Be understanding and kind.

What to do:
The next time you hear yourself beating yourself up aloud or in your head, stop it. You have to be able to recognize when you're being too hard on yourself and when you're giving in to negative thought cycles. Because those behaviors are toxic. They will not serve you or your purpose. So practice bigging yourself up. When things don't go the way you planned, give yourself a break. Think of how you would treat a friend in the same position, and offer yourself that same kindness, love, and support. Remember, human beings accomplish far more when they're being lifted up than they do when they're being put down. **A reward always motivates better than a punishment.** So keep your thoughts in the positive. Give yourself a break. Be good to yourself and accept that no one is perfect.

Don't forget, being good to yourself means allowing yourself the freedom to do the things that you love to do. A good percentage of your time should be spent on things that you value and enjoy. That includes who you spend your time with. If there are people in your life who you find to be draining and negative, limit the time you spend with them. Try to surround yourself with the people that make you feel good about yourself and the world in general. Prioritize the things that make you feel warm and fuzzy, ands keep the rest at arm's length.

10 - Don't let stress become a destructive force in your life.

"Knowledge is of no value unless you put it into practice."
Anton Chekhov

We all know that stress can bring out the worst in people. And it doesn't always make us behave in ways that we can be proud of. However, if we allow ourselves to lash out at the people we love, we could be alienating ourselves from them and making our relationships more difficult than they need to be. Of course, keeping everything inside isn't going to help much either. There is a difference between being kind to yourself and being horrible to other people and this is something that's important to consider if stress is causing difficulties in your relationships with others.

We all need to feel free and able to talk about the things that are upsetting us. And we truly do need to connect with other people. But if we become abusive, snide, or overly snippy with people, we run the risk of having to fight the battle alone. We need people by our side cheering us on, so we have to be careful not to alienate the people who love us. This is not an excuse to beat yourself up over every time you've taken things out on the wrong person. We all get a little out of hand sometimes and we do need to forgive ourselves and move on when that occurs. The thing is, it's often the people we're closest to who get exposed to our ugliest moments. Relationships are complicated. But there has to be an inner voice that can recognize when you're lashing out and give you the power to stop. Stress is awful and it's not easy to cope with, but it should not be given the power to destroy your life.

Later in this book I will discuss relationship difficulties and coping with conflict in greater detail. You will read about how stress can affect relationships but also how relationships can cause stress. For now though, focus on being kind to the people who give you the most love and support. Limit the amount of time you spend with people who tend to wind you up. Do your very best to leave work stress at work and home stress at home.

What to do:
If you think that stress may be bringing out the worst in you, take some time to think on it. Are there people who you have mistreated as a result of stress? Do you often take things out on the wrong person? Are you letting stress come between you and the people you love? This is not an easy topic to think about or to deal with on a

practical level. But when we give ourselves the chance to reflect on things, we're more likely to change the things that aren't working in our favor. There may be someone you need to apologize to. It could be someone at work, your mother, your partner… it could be you. You might need some time to figure out how to separate stress from the things that really matter. Maybe that means that you leave work at work instead of bringing it home. Maybe that means taking the time to tell someone that you appreciate his or her help, or rewarding yourself for getting through a difficult time.

Stress can be blinding. It can make us lose sight of the things that really matter to us. So it's important to think about this often rather than letting yourself bottle up and explode. It's important to recognize when things are starting to get out of hand so that you can slow them down and make sense of them. Talk to someone you trust and get things off your chest. We all need time to vent so we can recover and get our strength back for the next round. Many of the conflicts that we have with other people are preventable if we realize that we're getting worked up because of stress rather than getting worked up about things that really matter. Be careful about where you direct your negative energy. Try not to point it at yourself or other people. Consider exercising as a means to work it out of you. Consider trying out some relaxation techniques. Don't let stress be the ruler of your life. Remember it is hard enough to cope with these things without hating the person you've become. You are better than that and you are stronger than that.

11 - Keep a stress diary.

"The act of writing is the act of discovering what you believe."
David Hare

Traditional diaries aren't for everyone. While some of us benefit from writing out our daily comings and goings and the feelings attached to them, others prefer not to dwell on things and just carry on. But diaries can be of benefit to just about anyone if they're tailor made to suit their needs and their personality. There are stress diaries that you can purchase online or in bookstores. These will offer you guided writing exercises that can help you work out the feelings connected to your stress. They can be a very helpful tool not only for venting your frustrations but also for keeping track of how well you're coping with your stress. They can be a good place to come up with ideas for stress relief as well as making sense of your feelings.

But if you're not a big writer and keeping a diary feels awkward or unnatural for you, don't despair. There are plenty of other ways you can plot your progress. You can write every day if you want to but you don't have to. The easiest thing you can do, as I encouraged you to do earlier in this book, is to keep a simple daily journal rating your stress from 1 to 10, with 1 being the least stress and 10 being the worst. At the end of the day you simply ask yourself how good or bad your stress levels were that day and then write a single sentence or a couple of words about why you think that was.

As an example:
Monday, 4, Work was chaotic but things at home were great.
Tuesday 7, Mom was demanding but I didn't fall out with her.
Wednesday, 2, I finally finished my project and I'm really happy with how it turned out.

At the end of each week, you can count up your scores for the week and see how things progress over the month. Doing it like this means that you will also be able to see how some of your new coping mechanisms are working out. For instance, if you take on a gym membership and your number goes down, it's helping. But if your stress levels have gone up, you might need to try something else entirely or add something new into your regimen. Doing this will also help you identify your triggers. You will be able to see from your single sentence entries which things are causing you the most stress and which are getting easier. If you wrote about your mother six days in a row, you might need to address things with her. If work rates at the top of your list every week, it might be time to think about moving on or making some changes. One thing about stress is that it can make you tired. And when you're tired, your memory might not be as sharp. Keeping a diary is a way to keep track of things you might otherwise forget.

Finally, as I have warned you before, be careful with negative journaling. If you use your diary for negative things alone, you're likely to get yourself worked up and reach very few conclusions about positive change. So try to strike a balance in your diary or keep it entirely positive. Remember, this should be a tool for you to plot your progress and motivate yourself to keep making positive changes in your life.

What to do:
Think about what type of diary will work for you and get stuck in. Remember to choose something that will fit into your lifestyle. If you're likely to be exhausted by the end of the day, don't force yourself to write a fifty-page essay each night before bed. Remember that this is a tool designed to help you, not something to add extra things to your to do list. However you choose to journal your stress, make sure to include that daily 1-10 rating so that you can see clearly if things are getting better or worse. Life is complex, so having a diary to help you simplify and interpret the changes you put in place will be invaluable on your journey to serenity.

Use care with your journaling. It is possible to write too much. Specifically, be careful when writing about things that are currently upsetting you. Writing too much about negative things can have a negative impact on your mood. Remember that your diary is not a place for you to fall into the traps of obsessive or harmful thinking. When you're writing, try to strike a balance between positive and negative and if you feel like you're getting worked up or angry, put the journal away.

As you can tell, stress is something that needs management and prevention. It's not all about the moments when you feel like your head is going to explode. It's also the moments of self-doubt, worry, and sleepless nights. It's when you can't focus or concentrate, or you find yourself forgetting things that you normally wouldn't. Stress is often a daily experience, so putting daily preventative measures in place is an absolute must. The more you practice daily stress management, the lower your stress levels will be and the better you will be at coping with them. Remember that change takes time. So go easy on yourself. Slow and steady wins the race.

Dismissing The Worry

"Worry never robs tomorrow of its sorrow, it only saps today of its joy."
Leo Buscaglia

Like stress, worry is something we all experience throughout our lives; some to a greater extent than others. But although it's extremely common, worry can be quite complex. And when it comes to stress, worry can be a major contributing factor. So it's important that we all get to grips with our worrying tendencies in order to make sure that they are A) not a waste of our time and energy, and B) actually helping us to achieve something.

Worry is an enormously broad subject. By nature, it can worm its way into any part of life. In the span of a day, we can worry about when we're going to get the chance to get our grocery shopping done, what schools will be best for our kids, how we're going to find the money to fix our broken car, how to resolve a conflict at work, how to best help a sick relative, among countless other daily worries. None of these things are directly linked by any means, but worry does have a way of tying things together, often creating a tangled web of anxiety that's hard to break free from. If your stress levels are high, that web can become even more intricate and more difficult to find your way out of. A lot of us even worry about how worried we are! We stress out about how stressed out we are. But you have to remember that stress produces worry and worry produces stress, so it's important to figure out a way cut through that web so that you can *use* your worry to get things done rather than letting it freak you out and throw you off your game. It's all about turning your stress into fuel for your productive fire.

When we allow thoughtful consideration to turn into chronic worry, the negative effects are palpable. We find the days getting shorter and shorter because we're spending so much of our time fretting. We find it hard to concentrate, so things at work might take longer to accomplish than usual. We feel a rise in anxiety and may become short tempered around our friends and family. Most importantly, we start taking everything a little too seriously and losing the enjoyment and happiness we could feel within our lives otherwise. But many times, all it takes to break cycles of unproductive worry is a little bit of thought and self-reflection. There are plenty of people in the world who have shed their worrying tendencies in favor of productivity and positivity and there is no reason why you can't join them.

The best way to start thinking about how worry features in your life is by asking yourself a few questions. Self-reflection can be extremely beneficial if you get used to doing it. And if you train yourself to become good at it, it will help you better understand any number of things about yourself and how you approach life. There are no right or wrong answers here; these questions are really just prompts to get you thinking more deeply about your life and your habits. Remember that with knowledge comes power. The more you know and understand yourself, the better equipped you will be at improving your life. So ask yourself:

- Do you consider yourself to be a worrier?
- Do you think you worry too much?
- Do you feel like you're always short on time?
- Do you snap at people when they try to help or offer advice?
- Do you find it hard to stop worrying once you've started?
- Do you think you've been less productive as a result of worry?
- Do you spend more time worrying than you'd like?
- Do you ever gain anything positive from your worry?
- Do you feel like worrying is a productive force in your life or a destructive one?
- Is it possible that all worrying is doing is driving you crazy?

When we think of stress, it's important not to underestimate how much worrying can add fuel to the fire. But the *only* worry that should be allowed anywhere near your stress, is productive worry. Put simply, productive worry is that which you can put into immediate action. It's worry that you can do something with. For instance, let's say you have a driving test tomorrow. There are two types of worry that will be vying for your attention. One is unproductive and the other is productive.

The unproductive worry will lead you through a series of *"what ifs"*. It will not only lead you to think *"what if I don't pass"*, but it could also take you on a guided tour of every possible negative outcome that might happen as a result of not passing. You'll worry about how you're going to get to your family reunion since you were planning on driving there. You'll worry about the embarrassment you'll feel when you have to tell people that you've failed. You'll worry that you might have to take the test another time and what if you fail *again*? This type of worrying literally achieves nothing. It is a waste of time and energy that focuses entirely on negative possibilities. Not only are you more likely to have increased stress as a result, but you are also less likely to pass that test if your mind is swarming with negative potentialities.

On the other hand, productive worry - that is to say, the type that you can put into immediate action - is more likely to lead you to simply getting out on the road and practicing. Productive worry tells you to do what you can today, and toss the rest aside. Because in a case like this, worry will not only waste your time and energy, but it may also make you doubt yourself, and it can ramp up your anxiety so much that you'll end up failing because of your nerves alone.

What you need to conquer worry is perspective and level headedness. You need to be able to ask yourself, *"Is there anything I can do with this worry? Is this worry adding anything positive to this situation?"* If the answers to these questions are "no", stop it. Human beings can be very indulgent when it comes to mulling things over. We repeat scenes of how things *might* go over and over in our heads. We talk about our worries constantly or we stomach them and let them eat away at us. We focus on all possible outcomes when we have no control over a situation. We let worry cloud our vision and dictate how we handle things. Most importantly, we let it own our thoughts. Giving in to any of these habits is going to be bad news for your stress levels. Because the more you have to worry about, the worse your stress will become. Every little worry that's allowed to get under your skin is going to add another building block to your stress. The product of multiple insignificant worries is often insurmountable stress levels. Those building blocks may seem to be on the path to becoming a castle, until they all come tumbling down.

So how can you tackle unproductive worry and turn it into productive worry? The first thing to do is to think about what you can *do* with your worry. How can you turn your worry into action? For the driving test, you know that you can practice. If you're afraid that you might be ill, you could make an appointment to see a doctor rather than googling your symptoms and worrying about every possible ailment you might have. If you're worried about how your kids are doing in school, make an appointment to talk with their teachers rather than wringing your hands until report card day. If you're worried about a big house move, do some packing or make a few phone calls *today*. This is what productive worry looks like. You're taking your worry and putting it into immediate action so that you can feel like you've done everything you can do to solve your problems.

Another thing you can do to make your worry productive is to take control. Feeling helpless makes worry and stress harder to cope with, so if you're the type of person who tends to hang around waiting to see how things will turn out rather than getting stuck in, you're likely to worry even more during the waiting game. If you're waiting for a phone call when it would be just as easy and appropriate to make the call yourself, do it. Why sit around worrying when you can get an answer right now? Similarly, if you often let other people sort things out even though you know you could do them more effectively yourself, it might be time to grab hold of the reins. A lot of worry comes from lack of control; that is simply human nature. We all crave control over our lives and when we feel like things are out of our control we can get disoriented and emotionally activated. So if the things that you're worrying about are things that you can get control over, take it and run with it.

Next, and this is of upmost importance, learn to let go of the things you can*not* control. You have to recognize when you've done all you can do. This is extremely important when it comes to worry and stress. There is no point worrying or stressing out over things you cannot control or things you cannot change. Of course, this is easier said than done and it will take practice. Learning to be patient isn't always easy. If you're particularly wound up about something and your partner tells you to just let it go, you might feel like lashing out at them because they clearly cannot understand how much this thing is bothering you. But even though their words might seem insensitive or tactless at the time, they're probably right. Being able to let go takes practice. We are not all born with the same levels of patience. Some of us get worked up very easily while others are so laid back they're horizontal. But even if you are of the former mindset, there has to be a time when you tell yourself that enough is enough. It's time to retrain your thinking by recognizing when you're stressing out about something that's out of your control and forcing yourself to stop thinking and talking about it. Stop winding yourself up if it's out of your hands.

As a general rule of thumb, if you hear yourself complaining about the same thing more than once or twice a day, alarm bells should be ringing. Excessive complaining can be very dangerous when it comes to triggering stress and worry. The more we repeat ourselves, the more we are reminding ourselves of the negative forces in our life. We're telling ourselves to be angry over and over again. We are letting our worries and frustrations snowball. Excessive complaining can be toxic to you and those around you. So if this behavior sounds familiar, then learning to let go of the things you can't control is going to be of extreme importance for you.

"Complaining not only ruins everybody else's day, it ruins the complainer's day, too. The more we complain, the more unhappy we get."
Dennis Prager

Generally speaking, serenity isn't the easiest thing to achieve. Human life is steeped in unpredictability. It involves so many unknowns and so many possible frustrations. In many ways, the goings on in our lives can hold us in a constant state of limbo. We do a lot of waiting in life; waiting for phone calls, waiting for decisions, waiting to see how things will pan out at work or with a friend we're not getting along with. It's hard not to worry about things that are up in the air or unresolved. But when it comes to letting go of the things you have no control over, you can start by recognizing the difference between things that are *frustrating* and things that are truly *important*. That one bit of awareness could mean the difference between flying off the handle and losing time and energy to your peaking stress levels, or letting something wash over you with little more than a shrug. The difference is that things that are important will usually lend themselves to action, whereas things that are frustrating are more likely to lead towards complaining, stress, and general aggravation. So when you've got a lot of worries swarming around in your mind, ask yourself if each individual thing is important or if they're just annoying. This is a quick way of weeding out the unnecessary worries, thus lessening the quantity of your worries at least. Once you've shed the stuff that's not worth thinking about and you've decided not to dwell on those things anymore, you can address the things that are actually important by getting into action anywhere you can. Take each item one at a time rather than obsessing about how much you have to worry about and letting your mind spin out of orbit. Remind yourself to take it slowly. When you've got a lot on your plate, you're going to have better luck getting rid of it if you chip away at it. So try not to constantly focus on the whole plate, and consider each item individually instead.

Practice letting go of the things you can't do anything about. **Practice it as often as humanly possible.** Because that's what it takes to form healthy habits. When a worry pops into your head, set it aside and stay focused on doing what you're doing. When it pops up again, brush it to the side again. Practicing like this is building your ability to control your thoughts so that you can stay concentrated on the things the matter. This is also the way meditation teaches you to silence busy thoughts and simply be in the moment. You will hear me mention this way of gaining mind control throughout this book. For now, just keep practicing the act of hushing your worries when they arise. Be careful not to stomach them, or ignore things that really matter. Rather, recognize your thoughts, consider them, and if there's nothing you can do about them, let them go. Do this with every unproductive worry you have. I promise you, it will get easier the more you do this. Sometimes it's easier to create a visual aid as this can actually show us what we're doing with our worries. To do this, simply keep a couple of lists nearby. When something pops in your head, ask yourself if it is worth worrying about or not. If it isn't, put it on a No Worry list and when it comes to you again, remind yourself that it has already been considered and let it go again. If something is worth worrying about, put it on a Productive Worry list and write down anything you can do to solve it. Remember, the sooner you can solve a worry, the better. But if you cannot solve it today, then it's not worth worrying about. You can consider it again tomorrow.

Like I've said, very few of us are naturally serene. Achieving serenity is a skill. And it's the kind of skill that can have dramatically positive effects on your life. So, when there's something that you cannot take immediate action with, take the time to actively ask yourself, *"Is this worth my worry?"* Nine times out of ten, all your worry is doing is holding you back from being productive with other things. Ask yourself, *"Is this out of my control?"* If it is, let it go. Redirect your attention and move on. Ask yourself, *"Have I done everything I can do with this particular worry?"* If you have, **let it go**. Keep practicing and repeating this and soon it will become second nature.

Remember that you probably won't be able to do this all the time at the start. There will be times when you're just juggling too many things and struggling to cope with them all. But that's okay. Whatever you do, don't beat yourself up if you give in to worry. The last thing you need is to worry about worrying! Just remember that the more you practice letting go, the more you'll notice that things aren't bothering you quite so much. You'll be able to recover from worry faster. You'll find that the things other people do, won't stress you out as much. And most importantly, you'll find that you are able to get a lot more done and maintain a positive mental attitude for much longer. Life is a journey. It takes time and it has plenty of ups and downs. But believe in yourself and be brave about it.

Finally, if worry is a very strong force in your life, take a moment to ask yourself if you might be taking things a little *too* seriously. Are there certain things that you could stand to care a little less about? Do you dwell on things that don't really affect you or your life? Do you tend to blow things out of proportion or find problems where there aren't any? Worry is addictive and it's important that you realize that early on. The more things you worry about, the more things you will find to worry about.

Here are a few general rules to live by when it comes to worry:
1 - If it doesn't have anything to do with you…**let it go!**
2 - If it doesn't carry a major consequence…**let it go!**
3 - If you're in control of the situation…**let it go!**
4 - If someone else has everything under control…**let it go!**
5 - If you can't do anything about it…**let it go!**

The only things you should be worrying about are the things that you can take care of today. Worry is something that lives in the future and therefore, it belongs with everything else we cannot predict. No one knows what will happen tomorrow. That can either be terrifying or liberating and that's what you have to choose between. Do what you can do today and let yourself be light until tomorrow. You hold the power to do that.

What To Do:
Take 20 to 30 minutes to think about how worry features in your life. Ask yourself the following:

- Do you complain a lot about things you have no control over?
- Do you worry about things you can't do anything about?
- Can you recognize any ways in which worry is contributing to your stress?

Now, write a list of things that are worrying you or have been worrying you over the last few weeks. When you've finished writing, begin by crossing out anything which you have done all you can do to rectify as of today. There might be more you will be able to do on these things in the future, but if you've done all you can do today, cross it off the list. Next, look over the list and cross out anything that is out of your control. If it's out of your hands, it should be out of your thoughts. With the remaining items, circle the top three things that are worrying you the most and cross out the rest. Now rate your top three worries based on how important they are. Consider the rest of your worries off your plate for now. With those top three worries, write down *anything* you can do today or this week that will help resolve them. Then, get into action! When you've done all you can, let go of those worries until the situation changes.

This is a great way to prioritize your worries so that you can free up your brainpower for more productive and positive things. Do this any time you feel swamped or when you feel like you can't see the sun for the rain.

Beating Stress In the Moment

"Success is not final, failure is not fatal: it is the courage to continue that counts."
Winston Churchill

No matter how much we do to prevent stress and keep our stress levels in the mid to low range, there will always come times when stress comes barreling in our direction like a steam train. No matter how prepared we are, sometimes there's just no stopping it. Sometimes we take on too many projects at once, things at work become hectic, or we're just having a bad day, and in these moments it's important to have the skills and tools necessary to keep stress from wiping you out like a tsunami. Refer to this go-to guide any time your stress feels bigger than you or you feel like you're crumbling beneath the weight of it.

Defusing Stress As It's Happening

1 - Slow everything down.
Learning how to slow our thinking down is one of the greatest skills we can possess in life. It means not getting carried away, thinking obsessively, or making irrational decisions. When we're stressed out, our thoughts are more likely to run away with us. We're more likely to get worked up about how people treat us and we're less likely to be able to understand where other people are coming from. Racing thoughts are not uncommon but they can lead you into distraction and frustration when you need to be focused and calm.

The thing is, like most self-progression, learning to slow down your thoughts will take time and practice. Unfortunately, there is no quick fix. Later in this book I will discuss racing thoughts in light of conflicts and difficulties within your relationships. I hope to arm you with knowledge on the subject. But for now, there are things you can do to get into action.

A lot of times it's the hustle and bustle of life that is keeping our minds running at a thousand miles per hour. It's the adrenaline we're producing as we're rushing around trying to do too many things at once. It's the frustration and anxiety about upcoming projects that won't allow us to focus. Luckily, when your mind is racing, there is something you can do about it, and that is to simply *slow everything down*. When we're really busy it's easy to think that we have to keep moving fast in order to keep all the balls we're juggling in the air, but often all that does is create unrest, therefore hindering our production value. And sometimes the best way to quiet the mind, is to quiet the body. So, if your movement is creating a tornado, address it. Slow down your walking pace. Slow down the way you clean the house. Slow down the way you eat, how you drive, how you shower. And let your slow movements give your mind the break it needs to be able to think slowly, clearly, and productively. Once your body has slowed down, try to incorporate that reduced pace into your thinking. Do one thing at a time rather than multitasking to take a little bit of pressure off your brain. Again, you will read a lot more about the process of slow thinking as you progress through this book, but think of this as a step towards that inner peace you're craving. Hush your busy thinking and take one thing at a time.

2 - Get perspective.
Perspective is the ultimate key to inner peace and clear thinking. But when we're stressed out and emotions are high, it isn't always easy to achieve. We have to be able to see the bigger picture. We have to be able to accept that even when things are important, not everything means the end of the world. So when you feel like you're about to blow your lid, ask yourself what's the worst thing that could happen. Ask yourself:

- Will you be able to get through things even if they don't go perfectly?
- If the road isn't as smooth as you'd like it to be, does that mean you can't continue on your journey?
- Have you been in similar situations before and things worked out in the end?
- Have you coped with failure before?
- Will you cope with it again if need's be?

Asking yourself questions like this is a good way to begin slowing your thinking down and gain perspective on the situation at hand. You might want to bring some positivity into your self-talk. So think about the things that are going well. Think about how far you've come. Think about what things will look like when you finish this project or task.

Developing good self-talk habits will benefit you in all walks of life. The more you do it, the stronger you will become. Positive self-talk will also help replace any negative self-talk you may have ruminating in your mind. It'll help you recognize when you're stuck in negative cycles and help you turn them around. In a moment of heightened stress, positive self-talk and gaining perspective is like striking gold. It can make you a more patient and measured person. And that's who we need to be when we're facing stress.

3 - Stop talking and start doing.
Sometimes the best thing to do when you're feeling overwhelmed is to get into action. A lot of times the reason we get stressed out is because there's just too much to do. The problem is, when that is the case, a lot of us are more likely to either spin out completely or talk incessantly about everything that needs to be done. Falling into the trap of complaining can put a halt on your progress as well as having a terrible effect on your mood, your appetite, your sleep pattern…the list goes on and on!

So when you're in a tizzy, put that frantic energy to good use. Get working on anything you can do for now. Use stress as fuel to get you into action. If it seems like there's just too much to do and you can't focus on one thing, try writing a list. Lists give us a sense of control, they help us feel like we're on top of things and give us the satisfaction of holding the reins. In addition, lists can offer the simplicity and organization we need to get into gear. We can see what needs to be done more clearly, hence we can get to work and start crossing things off our list. This way, you know you're doing everything you can to get through your workload. You're not just talking about what you have to do. You're taking the adrenaline buzz and putting it to work.

4 - Get to the root of the problem.

There will always be things in life that are unpredictable and/or out of our control. However frustrating, this is an unavoidable evil in a lot of cases. Many times we have to wait for others to act before we can. We can't organize certain things until so-and-so does their part. And situations like that are stressful. However, this is not an excuse to let your emotions run away with you. When you have too much going on at once, it can be hard to identify what it is that's really bothering you. Instead of being able to pin point what's at the heart of it, we get caught up rhyming off things that need done and things that are driving us crazy. Often, even though it feels like there are tons of things that are weighing on you, beneath it all, there might only be one or two things that are really to blame.

Learning to identify what's really troubling you will give you the power to move on. This isn't always the easiest thing to do but it is always worth it. A lot times, there's one thing on your to do list that's heavier than the rest and that can be pretty easy to identify and move forward with. Other times, things aren't that simple. In your conscious mind you may be going over and over your to do list or worrying about upcoming tasks and events, but deep down, something else is troubling you. At the foundation of your stress, there might be something you actually hadn't noticed. For instance, you may have feelings of disappointment or pain from a conversation you had with a friend. You might still feel hurt after a break-up. Beneath it all, you might be worried about your health. At the root of your problem, you might be having a moment of insecurity or self-doubt.

These things are often hidden by the flurry of life. They are things that aren't easy to face but they can eat you from the inside out if you continue to ignore them. For this reason, taking the time to reflect on your feelings is extremely important when stress has a hold on you. A lot of times, all we need to do is acknowledge our underlying concerns and feelings in order to move on. Sometimes we just need to cry or let ourselves feel angry. Taking time to get to the root of the problem might take bravery and it could make you emotional. However, once you've gotten to the root, the rest of your stress can die down and be uprooted like a weed. So when times are tough, try to get some quiet time for perspective and introspection. Cut through the noise and get to the foundation of what's really bothering you. Be brave enough to face it. Talk to someone you trust. Feel your feelings. Then take a deep breath and move on.

5 - Fresh air and 5/7 breathing.
As simple and obvious as it sounds, sometimes we just need to cool off when things are heating up. If you're in a moment of heightened stress and you're having a hard time slowing things down, go outside and *breathe*. Take a walk or a drive. Give yourself plenty of time to steady your mind and calm down before you face your problems again. You can use 5/7 breathing anywhere at any time, although I would encourage you to get out of the stressful environment if at all possible. 5/7 breathing simply means breathing in for 5 long seconds and breathing out for 7. You won't believe how much this type breathing can help talk you down off a ledge. Try it now to see how it affects your mood and your focus. Doing even a single 5/7 breath could stop you from melting down while helping you gain control of yourself. This is especially helpful if you are having an argument or a conflict. If you've got a temper or you're likely to blow, 5/7 breathing and some fresh air could be all you need to calm down.

You have to know when to walk away, and a good rule is, if you're likely to say or do something you'll later regret, leave it for now and go cool off. It's okay to be disappointed when things don't go your way. But you have to know when to let go. If you can't use your disappointment for good, get some air.

But 5/7 breathing can of course also help when you're just feeling swamped. If you have too much to do or your thoughts are racing, 5/7 breathing can give you a chance to push the reset button. You can take this breathing a step further by saying a mantra aloud or in your head. Something like *"right here, right now, everything is fine"* can get your mind centered in the present. This is especially helpful if you're worrying about something that may or may not happen in the future, or if you're dwelling on something that already has happened which you can't do anything about. Saying *"let go"* as you breathe in an out is a great way to help you strip away the frustrating stuff so that you can focus on the important stuff. Think *"let"* as you breathe in for 5 counts, and *"go"* as you breathe out for 7 counts.

"I can, I will" is a good mantra for motivation and beating self-doubt. Think *"I can"* as you breathe in for 5 counts, and *"I will"* as you breathe out for 7. Of course, you can tailor make mantras for yourself and this might be something you want to think about when you're already in a state of calm or relaxation. This can help better prepare you for those moments when you need a quick fix.

6 - Ask for help.
You might notice that I mention this a lot and there's good reason for it. It's not always easy to admit that things are getting out of hand. Acknowledging that you can't do everything alone can feel like you're admitting defeat. You might feel disappointed in yourself, or you may be too proud to acknowledge that disappointment at all. But the thing is, when we don't ask for help we're only hurting ourselves. We're setting ourselves up for either failure or a breakdown. I have already mentioned the importance of taking care of number one and this is a prime example of a time when you need to put that into action. If you're stressed up to your eyeballs, you won't be doing anyone any good by insisting on doing everything yourself. It takes a big person to ask for help, but doing so doesn't mean that you've failed. Rather, it means that you know how to use your resources wisely. It means that you're saving your energy for the big stuff by delegating the little stuff to other people.

But asking for help isn't just about delegating tasks. It's also about waving a white flag. There will be times when you'll just need to take a break. You'll need to take a day off work to rest, or you'll need to talk to a friend about things that are troubling you. It's important to have a forum to talk about things when you're feeling overwhelmed. This doesn't mean that you have to be a drain on your loved ones; it just means that when the going gets tough, you can ask for some support either logistically or emotionally. Sometimes all we need is to get things off our chest. Other times we need someone to cover for us so we can get a little head space. Sometimes we just need a hug and a word of encouragement. These are not moments of failure. They are merely moments of humanity. They are moments that we will all experience at one time or another. Please remember that being able to ask for help is a strength, not a weakness.

7 - Recognize when you've done enough.
One of the hardest things about managing stress is knowing when to let go of it. Stress is a distracting force. It can mess with your moods, your memory, your ability to concentrate, and your overall productivity. Although every scenario is different, stress often arises when we've taken on too many things at once or we just have too much to do in a short amount of time. The problem with times like these is that having so many tasks happening at once can have a dizzying effect on us. When we're not flying off the handle, stress is still simmering in our guts. This is why we can't sleep at night. This is why our relationships are strained. This is why we're low on patience. But, it doesn't have to be any of those things.

When we're able to recognize that we've done all we can, we will naturally be more able to let go of stress. Sure, there may be things that aren't fully finished and projects that will span over long periods of time. But, if you know that you've done everything you can do on a particular task today or this week, you must acknowledge that truth and release yourself from the stress attached to that task. When we fail to do this, these tasks and the stress attached to them, act as building blocks in our minds. They continue to increase the amount of pressure we're under. They keep us in a state of frantic, heightened stress. So when you're feeling overwhelmed, take a half an hour to look at everything you have going on. Identify any tasks where you've done as much as you can for now, and visualize yourself letting go of them and the emotions they carry. Things that you have already accomplished should bear no weight. When you've done all you can, you are allowed to let things go. If not, you'll only become wrapped up in unproductive worry.

What to do:
Over the next few days or weeks, try some of these tactics out when you're feeling flustered. Use your diary to write down things that worked for you and things that didn't really help. Remember to keep rating your stress from 1 to 10 daily so you can keep a close eye on your progress. If something isn't quite working for you, try tweaking

it to suit yourself better. If it's not working for you at all, let it fall by the way side! Remember that these ideas are not here to add extra stress or more things to do! These are coping mechanisms to help you slow things down and get a hold of yourself when stress is high. Don't forget that stress is a very broad subject and we are all individuals. We are allowed to tailor make our coping strategies to fit our own individual needs. Do what works for you and don't worry if there are ideas here that don't quite fit into your life. The object of the game is to improve *your* coping skills and *your* life. This book is here to guide you, but you're the one in control.

Free Ourselves From The Hands Of Stress

"Fall down seven times, get up eight."
Japanese Proverb

No matter how many lists of practical tips and motivation I provide you with throughout this book, if you really want to get rid of stress for good, you'll need to get to the cause of it eventually. We all need to dig a little deeper if we want to truly free ourselves from the hands of stress. For most of us, there isn't going to be just one single thing at the root of the problem, but rather many things of varying importance and magnitude. It can be hard to see through the fog. It can be hard to understand why we feel the way we do. It is frustrating when we get stressed out about little things; we may get angry at ourselves for getting worked up over nothing or we might worry that there is something more sinister at work. And yes, sometimes there is something bigger going on, like depression, and if that is the case, it will obviously need to be addressed. Depression and stress have been known to go hand in hand. Stress itself, can cause things like depression and mood swings, and depression can cause stress. However, it would be naive to assume that stress is merely a mask for depression for everyone. We all experience stress, regardless of our mental health. But if you're committed to getting rid of stress for good, you might need do some self-exploration in order to get to the bottom of it. There are countless things that could be causing your stress levels to rise or hang around longer than you'd like. In this section, I will narrow these things down to a few common causes of stress that most of us face throughout life. There should be a number of relevant ideas here for every reader to benefit from.

In today's world, most of our lives are fast paced, and it can be hard to find a sense of inner peace when we're surrounded by chaos. For whatever reason, most of us are constantly busy these days. Some of us are workaholics, others like the buzz we get from adrenaline, and plenty of us simply have no choice in the matter. You already know from reading up to this point that being contactable at all times doesn't help stress. You know that having no structure in your life and staring at screens all day prevents your mind from achieving a stable foundation. It makes you tired and impatient. But what about the chaos that's out of your control? What about your racing thoughts or general restlessness? What about the times you forget things or struggle to concentrate?

We can start tackling these things by slowing everything down and taking one thing at a time. Remember that racing thoughts and self doubt are big contributors where stress is concerned, so think about some ways you can cut through them. When you can't get a hold on your thoughts, close your eyes and do some 5/7 breathing. Train your brain to silence the things you have no control over and the things that are currently in limbo. Practice this every day. As soon as you hear yourself worrying or stressing out about things that are out of your hands, recognize it and stop it. Tell yourself that your brain energy could be put to better use. Focus on doing one task at a time when your mind is in this type of flurry. Multitasking is great when you're in good form but it doesn't help when your head is spinning. Remember to slow your physical movements down as well. Get perspective on the matter and ask for help wherever possible. Even when things seem to be of extreme importance today, ask yourself how much they will matter in the long run.

What will happen if things don't get done the way you'd like them to today?
Will it create a long-term problem or a short-term problem?
Will anyone get hurt?
Will you be able to recover, even if that means having to put in a little extra work?

When we take the time to ask ourselves questions like this, we are actively talking ourselves off the stress cliff. Self-reflection can be a lifesaving habit if you practice it enough. Being able to slow down your thoughts and bring yourself back down to earth is a skill that all of us can benefit from, so keep at it. Keep practicing.

Remember that organization is a total stress buster because it brings order to the things that are stressing us out. So when things are particularly hectic, try to keep all the things you're in charge of well organized. If you're in a heightened state, you might benefit from taking a half hour to write some lists or rearrange your schedule for the week. It could be time well spent. Once you've slowed down your thinking and gotten yourself organized, do your absolute best to keep your stress compartmentalized. By this I mean to keep work at work and home at home. Try not to bring work stress into the household, and when times are tough on a personal level, do your best to shield yourself from it when you need to be productive at work. Don't stomach the stress so it'll rear its ugly head later, just set it to one side when it's time to focus on other things.

One thing I'd like to discuss here is something called *imposter syndrome*. Whether you've heard of it or not, this is something that most people will feel at one point or another in their lives. It may strike when you're feeling low or when things are particularly stressful, but other times it can come out of nowhere. You might have it all the time or it may come and go. Put simply, imposter syndrome is an intrusive thought that makes you believe you're a fraud, despite any evidence working against that theory. It is usually accompanied by a fear of being *"found out"* or exposed. It can range from fleeting moments of self doubt to full blown negative self beliefs despite one's intelligence, success, or any other evidence of being an entirely competent individual. Imposter syndrome can affect just about anyone, but more often than not, it is experienced by people who have achieved highly in life or who have high-powered careers. It feels as though you don't deserve to be where you are in life or as though you've been faking it the whole time.

Another common facet of imposter syndrome is an inability to recognize when you've done something worthy praise or reward. You may put things down to luck or consider it a fluke when things go your way, even if you've put a lot of hard work and expertise into the project at hand. You'll either experience these moments spontaneously and sporadically, or you might chronically feel as though you're faking your way through life and someone could *"figure you out"* at anytime. But imposter syndrome isn't your brain telling you that you're actually faking. It's just flagging up something deeper, like self-doubt, uncertainty, guilt, high stress levels, or anxiety regarding future success. If you ask a bunch of your friends if they've ever felt this way, chances are most or all of them will have experienced this at some point, and knowing that can be quite comforting. But if we take the time to look at imposter syndrome more deeply, if we really dig into it, we'll usually find just a few things at the foundation, and they are: a fear of rejection, a need for approval, and/or feelings of inadequacy.

"Approval is a lover who will always break your heart."
Sammy Rhodes

Rejection, approval, and inadequacy can be seriously stressful tormenters. We all need to be approved of. No matter how strong our exterior is, knowing that someone appreciates you, respects you, and looks up to you is food for the soul. It's the thing that makes us stop feeling like imposters and gives us a chance to fully own our successes. We all require validation in order to carry on doing what we're doing and if we don't get that, it's only natural that we will begin to doubt our abilities and purpose in life. Our need for approval begins in childhood and stays with us for most of our lives. It's an important building block to our self-esteem, our identity, and our feelings of belonging within society. Without sufficient approval from others, we can develop feelings of being different, out casted, or simply not good enough.

Rejection shares many similarities with the absence of approval. It can pull the rug right out from under your feet no matter how strong you felt beforehand. It too, can make us doubt ourselves and our capabilities. It can make us feel shame and embarrassment, even when we have no real reason to feel that way. It can wreak havoc on our self-esteem. The thing about rejection is that it's quite a broad subject when you think about it. We don't just reel rejected when we're not chosen to be someone's companion. We feel rejection when we've worked hard at something and fail to get recognition for it. We feel rejection when we create something that people respond negatively or indifferently too. We feel rejection when people don't notice changes that we've made in our lives. And of course, we feel rejection when we really care about something and the people in our lives are unsupportive of it. Feelings of rejection can torment the mind.

In addition to the pain of rejection, feeling inadequate can also have detrimental effects to our self-image and confidence. It holds us back from taking risks. It makes us feel like we don't belong to be where we are; that everyone else is better or more worthy than us and that we have no place among our peers. We might become bitter or resentful of the people who surpass us in life. We might become jealous or disappointed in ourselves. And we're likely to find it hard to progress in life for fear of failure. As I'm sure you know or can imagine, these feelings are toxic. They feed imposter syndrome and stress, so you have to break free from them.

The Secret Beast We Must Slay

Here's three ways you can smash through your imposter syndrome and keep your head in the game:

1 - Stop trying to keep up with the Joneses.
You have to stop comparing yourself to others. You must to be able to judge yourself by your own criteria rather than judging yourself based on the successes and lives of others. Your values and desires do not have to match everyone else's. What matters is that you allow yourself to appreciate the things that you like about your life. There may be things about you or your life that don't live up to other people's standards. But if those things are enough for you, that's all that matters. Look at your past as the background of your current life.

How did you get where you are today?
Did you overcome obstacles?
Have you survived hard times?
Don't you deserve credit for getting this far?

We have to be able to approve of ourselves if we're ever going to get anywhere in life. This can be hard for people who have had difficult pasts. If you feel as though one or both of your parents never approved of you as a child, you're likely to find it hard to approve of yourself in adulthood. If you've always come in second place, you're probably in need of a self-esteem boost. But you have to be able to do that for yourself. You have to be able to look at your accomplishments with pride. Every time you have overcome an obstacle in life, you have proven to yourself that you are worthy of praise and approval. Focus on your achievements and hold onto them when imposter syndrome tries to knock you down. Do something nice for yourself when you've risen to a challenge. It doesn't matter how big or small your accomplishments are. You may have simply gotten through a tough day. But being able to recognize that and reward yourself means that you are actively approving of yourself. You are changing any bad habits that could be causing you to experience imposter syndrome or stress. Practice doing this and commit yourself to making it a habit because it's one that will serve you well in life.

Being able to approve of yourself can lift you up after a fall and prop you up on days you're not at your best. Practice by reflecting on your accomplishments each day. Force yourself to end the day by writing down three or more things that you have done well today. It may seem like a frivolous exercise but doing this gives you an opportunity to pat yourself on the back. We need to be able to encourage ourselves, not just doubt ourselves or put ourselves down. Self-approval can be the hardest approval to gain, but when we have it, so many of our fears disappear.

2 - Look at the evidence.
When you're caught up in negative thought cycles brought on by imposter syndrome, it's easy to think that you don't belong where you are. It's easy to get lost in thoughts of inadequacy. Negative thoughts are a part of life but they're not the easiest things to tame. Sometimes you need a weapon to cut through them, and that's where evidence comes in. When you get the fear, take a moment to think about why you are where you are.

How did you get here?
Has your life experience helped you to get to this point in life?
What have you done in the past that might help prove to yourself that you're good enough?

What skills, knowledge, and expertise do you have?
Are there things you can do better than anyone else can?

Look at how you got to this moment and big yourself up. Whether you studied for years at university or you made something out of nothing, there is a reason you have the things you do.

You have overcome difficulties in the past; this means you *are* resilient.
You have stuck with things to the end; this means you *are* dedicated.

You have learned and grown throughout your life. That means that you can continue to do so. Talk yourself off that ledge by looking at your accomplishments through positive, honest eyes, not doubtful ones. Let the evidence show that you deserve the good things in your life. Take ownership and pride in that thought.

3 - Rise up!
In life, we have to be able to use our negative emotions as fuel. If you feel inadequate today, do something to prove that you're not. If you feel like you don't approve of yourself right now, do something that will harvest that approval. Fix something that didn't go as you planned. Challenge yourself. Face a fear. If you're afraid of failing, take a risk. We do not get enough time on this earth to waste it all on self-doubt. There is no time for self-pity or self-loathing. There is only time to get better and do better. Take your negative feelings and all your fear and turn them into **fire**. Be the person you want to be. Be the person that you can approve of. Because why be anything else?

The next thing you might want to consider as a potential background of your stress is a certain type of addiction. I'm not talking about alcohol or substance abuse, but rather I'm suggesting that those of us with addictive personalities can become addicted to specific *feelings*. When you're thinking about stress and what lies beneath it, is it possible that you could be addicted to adrenalin? We've all heard the phrase "adrenalin junkie" and usually it's used regarding people who enjoy extreme sports and adventure. But leaping from a plane isn't the only way to get your heart pounding. Being late to a meeting can actually do the same thing. It is very possible that people who are perpetually late to work or other obligations are living in a state of adrenalin buzz. Because rushing around with the fear of being late kicks us into overdrive. Someone with habits like this is likely to find it hard to relax. They might pace around the house a lot, cleaning and fixing things rather than sitting down and taking a break. They might be constantly rushing around, trying to do too much at once, and unable to get their feet back on solid ground.

When we're high on adrenalin, our minds and bodies are naturally going to be in heightened states. Adrenalin gets us worked up. We can't concentrate or slow our thinking down. We can't focus on one task because we're too activated. We might feel anxious or impatient. Most importantly, when we're in this state our stress levels could be through the roof. If you're addicted to adrenalin, you might be in that heightened state a lot. You might not take sufficient time to wind down and relax. You might feel constantly on edge. Take some time to think about your own behavior and habits.
Do you feel like you're constantly on the go?
Are you often worked up or do you feel like you're "buzzing" a lot?
Do you think adrenalin plays a role in your stress?

If so, you might want to consider some relaxation exercises such as yoga or meditation. You might benefit from using some lavender oil on your pulse points or in a diffuser in your home. Lavender oil is great when it comes to getting your body and mind to slow down and relax. Taking substantial time away from screens will also help to steady your mind and bring you back to earth. As I have said again and again, you should aim to have screen-free time and quiet time every single day. Your body and mind need a chance to recover from the adrenalin coursing through your veins. If you are often running late, spend the next couple of weeks getting rid of that habit. Running around like a headless chicken isn't good for anybody, especially where stress is concerned.

Another thing that could be beneath your stress is an inability to cope with frustration. We all know what it feels like when things don't go our way, and more importantly, we know what it's like when things are up in the air, so to speak. Times of change and transition can be hard on the mind. Whether you're in between jobs, you're moving house, you're retiring, or waiting for the arrival of a new baby, it's easy to become frustrated when things are unpredictable. Living in limbo isn't easy. Things that are out of our control can be maddening. A change of plans could totally throw you off your game. None of these things are particularly pleasant, but if you have a hard time coping with them, it's only natural that your stress levels will increase.

When dealing with frustration, we have to be able to let go. We need to be able to silence our unproductive worries and focus on other things while we're waiting for the dust to settle. Relaxation techniques will be of great help to those who are easily worked up by frustration. Yoga, meditation, acupuncture, 5/7 breathing, and the use of calming essential oils will be of great benefit. But there are other things you can do to temper the effect that frustration has on you. First, don't allow yourself to overthink things. A lot of times when we're in a period of transition or things are just frustrating in general, it's easy to worry about every possible outcome, but doing so is only going to stress you out more. There is no point in worrying about things that may or may not happen in the future. Nor is there any point in dwelling on things that have already happened. Your energy is much better spent here in the present. If you are prone to overthinking things or talking obsessively about them, try setting a timer for yourself. Give yourself 3 to 5 minutes to consider the things that are frustrating you and when the timer goes off, stop it. You have to be able to set limits for yourself if you're likely to let your frustrations run away with you.

Second, do your best to think positively. Dwelling on the negative side of things can be seriously detrimental to your mood and how you relate to the people around you. We have to be careful that we don't drain people with our negative energy, and that includes ourselves. Negativity takes a lot out of us. It's heavy. And the more we indulge in it, the stronger it gets. So when you feel yourself dwelling on the negative, you've got to learn to cap it. When you need to turn it around, try writing down five things that you like about yourself or your life. Simple exercises like this work far better than you'd imagine. When you need a quick attitude adjustment, take yourself out of the negative environment for ten minutes, and spend that time thinking about things that you're happy about. Our moods are obviously going to be affected by what's happening around us, but if you have the power to summon up some positivity, why waste it?

In times of frustration, ask yourself if you might be taking things a little too seriously. Remember that life is for living. We need to be able to enjoy it and have fun. Get some perspective on the thing that's frustrating you. Is this something that's going to still be bothering you in a few years? A few months? Will you even care about it next week? If this is something that's going to pass, like most things do, tell yourself to relax and lighten up. Shift your focus elsewhere. Ask yourself if this thing is really worth all the trouble it's causing you. Is being frustrated helping the situation at all? Is it carrying negativity into other parts of your life? If so, is it worth it? Do your best to let go if you can't control the situation. Do something to blow off steam. Play a game with your family, get some exercise, take a walk to clear your head. Prioritize your enjoyment of life. Because very few things are worth taking that away from you.

Self-reflection gives us a chance to look inward and question our thoughts and behavior. Introspection is important for self-growth. The more we know about ourselves, the better we can become. The more we understand our triggers and our weaknesses, the stronger we will eventually feel. There is no substitute for self-knowledge and understanding. We are never done growing up. We can use our adulthood as a platform to grow from now until the day we die. So remember, no matter what you're struggling with, be it stress, a break up, or a period of low mood, there is always a way out. You just have to start by looking inward.

Simplify Your Life Without Losing Out!

"The ability to simplify means to eliminate the unnecessary so that

necessary may speak."
Hans Hofmann

It doesn't take a rocket scientist to know that most things in life will be easier to cope with if we break them down into their simplest forms. If we're able to strip things back to basics we will naturally be able to think and act more clearly and more effectively. But life in today's world isn't simple. It's complex. It's muddled up. We're doing too much. We're thinking too much. There's just too much to focus on. The good news is, you don't have to move to remote destinations in order to get some peace and quiet. No matter what your life is like, there is always room for simplification. When it comes to stress, simplifying your life can help you get your head out of the clouds and get your feet back on solid ground. In order to simplify things, you can implement changes in virtually every aspect of your life or just alter a few minor things. Think of it as spring-cleaning for the mind. In life, you have to know what's important to you. You have to know what gives your life value so you can focus on those things instead of focusing on the things that make you frustrated or overwhelmed. You have to be able to silence the noise in life, and simplifying is a great place to start. Here's a list of ways you can invite simplicity and eliminate complexity in your everyday life.

1 - Tackle household clutter.
Whether you've got a few things lying around the house that you've been meaning to get rid of or you're a moment away from being a guest on the hit TV show *Hoarders*, living with items that hold no use or value is bad for the mind. Household clutter robs you of the clear physical space you need when you're stressed out. Having too much to look at makes it harder to think clearly. Having cupboards, closets or rooms that are in dire need of a clear out can weigh us down when we're not even aware of it. It's stuff that even if it's not on your *active* to do list, it's still been on your *eventual* to do list for too long.

Designate a day of your time to sift through your clutter. Don't try to do it on a day when you're stretched for time, as this will make this exercise stressful rather than cleansing. Organize your clutter into piles of things that you can sell, things that you can give to a friend, things you can give to charity, and things that need to be thrown away. Avoid the temptation to hold on to things that you *"might need one day"*, because that is exactly what clutter is! If you've had things that you've been planning on using for a year or more and you still haven't, get real and get rid of it. If you have a box of old plugs, cords, and remote controls that you haven't touched since 1989, throw them away. If your kids have grown out of toys, clothes and games, gift them or sell them. Create rules for sentimental items to avoid unnecessary attachment. For example, let yourself hold on to one or two of your favorite items of baby clothes rather than keeping your kids' entire wardrobes.

In the kitchen, start by getting rid of any food that has expired. Then attack things you've been holding onto needlessly. For instance, that packet of seaweed you bought eight months ago when you thought it'd be cool to make your own sushi. If you haven't opened it yet, you probably never will! Donate items that fall into this category to a local food bank. Tackle the refrigerator next. Declutter, clean, and organize it. Clear your countertops of any appliances that you don't use daily. Get into your medicine cabinet and throw away anything that has expired. Get rid of body lotions and bath bombs that you haven't touched in years. Things like this may feel like they take a lot of time and energy but it will have a massive effect on your mood and your stress levels. Clutter weighs us down when we need to feel light.

2 - Plan your week.
There's nothing worse than being stressed out by the little things in life. A lot of times when we have a heavy work load or we're in the midst of a difficult time, the idea of school runs, laundry, and figuring out what to cook for dinner can throw you over the edge. The human mind can only cope with making so many decisions each day, and that doesn't just include big decisions. It also includes what you're going to wear for the day, when and where you're going to do your weekly grocery shop, what you're going to have for breakfast, etc.

Decisions rule our lives but if we're not careful, they can run us into the ground. So rather than ending up going ballistic over dirty dishes, simplify things beforehand to prevent that meltdown. If your week generally starts on a Monday, use Sunday as planning day. Write out meal plans and chore lists for the week ahead. Include all meals including the stuff you put in your kids' lunch boxes. Write your grocery list at the same time so you'll be sure to have all the ingredients you'll need during the week and you won't waste money on things you're not going to use. Planning meals is a fantastic way to save money on top of reducing your daily decisions, so give it a try.

Make a list or chart of household chores. Designate a few jobs for everyone in the household. If you're prone to cleaning the kids' rooms, take yourself out of that equation and let them handle it themselves. Ask your partner to prepare half the meals during the week to take some pressure off you. If you're the only one in the house, divide your list up so that you have a smaller list for each day instead of trying to clean the whole house after work one evening. Remember to take into account what clothes you'll need throughout this week and next. Don't forget about items that may need to be dry cleaned or ironed. Don't forget your kids' swimsuits and PE clothes. Include everything you possibly can in your plan so that your mind is free of this stuff during your work week.

I can't stress enough how important planning is when it comes to reducing stress. Planning and making decisions ahead of time means freeing up your mind for larger, more important tasks. There is no point in getting worked up over the little things if you have the power to prevent that from happening. Finally, if you have things that have been on your to do list forever, just cross them out. They are clearly not important enough to prioritize, which means they're not important enough to stress you out.

3 - Re-evaluate your relationships.
This can be a difficult subject to approach but many times, what lies beneath stress is conflict and difficult relationships. Later in this book you will find a section about dealing with conflict and overcoming difficulties like these; however, despite the complexity

of relationships in general, there are times when things are pretty much black and white. Relationships do not just include those we share intimacy with. Rather for the purpose of this argument, relationships include friends, family, co-workers, people you run into at school or at the gym, and any other people you communicate with on a semi-regular basis.

There are many reasons we might choose to stay close to people even when things aren't great between us. Sometimes we can't avoid it, other times we feel emotionally obligated to be there for someone despite the fact that they're never there for us. But there is no need to remain attached to people who are not adding value to your life. If there are people in your life who drain you or treat you poorly, you should not feel obligated to remain in a relationship with them. Sometimes, we've got to make cuts in our friend groups and this is never easy, especially if you're not a fan of confrontation. This doesn't mean you have to make a big commotion about it or cut people out of your life completely. You can set a few boundaries that could make things a lot easier. This might include only being available for someone at set times of the week. For instance if you have a friend who distracts you with emails or texts all day long, you can either tell them directly that you need them to ease up a bit or simply stick to replying a specific amount of times each day or week and they'll soon get the hint.

Another important boundary to have in place is knowing what subjects you're happy to discuss with whom. We all have people in our lives who can be insensitive and judgmental. You might feel tied to a person like this because they are a close relative or they're someone you like a lot despite their negative qualities. But with people like this, you have to be careful. If you're stressed out and you call them to get things off your chest, they're likely to say things that are not only unhelpful, but that might actually hurt your feelings and leave you feeling worse. If you regularly get off the phone with someone feeling frazzled and worked up, you probably need to put a boundary in place. One of the easiest ways to do this is by simply not talking to that person about things they will not understand or things they are likely to be unsupportive about. If someone in your life is overly critical of you and the choices you make, don't tell them what you're up to! Talk about something else. Ask them questions about them rather than opening your heart for a potential stabbing. When you need to talk about something close to your heart, choose the people you feel emotionally safe with.

Ultimately, if someone is not adding value to your life or they often leave you feeling emotionally depleted, limit your contact with them. Take a break from someone if you don't want to cut them out of your life completely. Remember that you're allowed to say no. If someone is taking too much from you and keeps asking you for favors, you can say no. If the gang at work wants you to join them for drinks on Friday and you don't particularly enjoy things like that, you're allowed to say no. You are not obligated to give your time and energy to anyone who is going to leave you feeling empty or negative.

4 - Get organized.
You have heard me say this before, but organization is paramount to lowering stress levels. But it can be a vague term until you put it into action. As human beings, we are diverse and it is our individual experiences that should dictate how we organize our lives. But there are a few things everyone can do to maintain order and control in their daily comings and goings. First of all, find a to do list system that works for you. You can do this on paper or get an app for your mobile phone. There are a lot of great tools like this available online. I suggest creating separate lists for each part of your life and each day of the week. Doing this creates lists that are achievable and much less daunting than having everything on one big list. This means you won't be stressed out about what you have to do tomorrow while you're looking at today's list. A lot of times when we're stressed out, we keep thinking about all the things we have to do in the coming days and weeks. This type of thinking is unhelpful as it ramps up your stress making it harder for you to concentrate on what you need to work on today. Of course, it's always a good idea to use your time wisely. And if there's something you can get done today with relative ease, you may as well do it instead of waiting until tomorrow.

Second, get your paper work in order. This is something that's worth spending time on as most households have a table by the front door or in the kitchen that serves as a dumping ground for letters and bills. Have a specific place for bills, medical papers, school stuff, etc. We all know what it's like searching for a specific letter amongst a stack of papers: it's stressful! So prevent that future meltdown by keeping things organized. Designate a time to sort your papers once a week or every other week. Don't wait until your pile of papers is three feet high! Try to go "paperless" with your bills wherever possible as well. You might also want to consider putting a sign by your mailbox if you don't want to receive flyers and other junk mail.

Lastly, keep your online activity as streamlined as possible. If you have multiple email addresses, sync them up to save yourself the time you'd otherwise spend signing into all of them multiple times every day. If you get a lot of spam or unwanted emails from services and websites, take some time to unsubscribe to them. There is usually a link at the bottom of emails like this that can unsubscribe you in one or two clicks. Use it! Remember to set designated times to read and respond to texts and emails each day so that you don't become distracted by incoming messages when you're trying to get things done. Try to avoid social media when you're working. There are apps that you can set to block certain websites during designated hours which can be very helpful for those of us who tend to scroll through news feeds when we're meant to be working. Most of us feel a significant drop in our stress levels when we're getting things done. So do everything you can to block distractions while you're on task.

5 - Get to the point.
Keeping communications simple can cut through tension and stress like a hot knife through butter. The more we put things off or dance around subjects, the longer we draw things out and the more our stress levels rise. When you're dealing with decision making - whether you're trying to manage tasks at work or you're just trying to organize a night out with friends - the easiest way to come to a conclusion is to be upfront. Say what you mean and get to the point right from the start. It's great to be open to ideas but if you're the type of person who rarely says no or sets boundaries, not being able

to be assertive could be making your communications with others more stressful than they need to be.

A lot of times we worry about being rude. We don't want to be bossy or to put anyone else out, but we have to strike a balance where communication is concerned. For instance, if you need a favor from a friend, don't beat around the bush and hope they're going to offer help. Just be straight with them. If there's something you need help with at work or at home, let yourself delegate with confidence. If there's something that you're trying to sort out via text or email, be especially clear about it. Because why go back and forth twenty times when you can get things done in two or three messages? People respond well to clear, honest leadership. Remember that you don't need to be apologetic about being assertive. You don't have to be rude about it, just forthright.

When we're not assertive with our needs, things get complicated. We're much more likely to become upset when people don't do what we need them to do. And even more detrimentally, we're likely to behave with passive aggression. It's important to keep your head out of the sand. It's important to stop beating around the bush. Keep things simple by just being upfront and honest.

What To Do:
Simplifying your life is a process. It will take some time to get everything in order so try not to worry about it or attempt to change too much at once. If you are particularly busy, consider doing one thing each week to move towards a simpler life. Get rid of your old clothes one week, sell some stuff on eBay the next week. Remember that change isn't always easy and it doesn't always happen overnight so go easy on yourself and try to take one thing at a time.

Start getting used to planning your weeks ahead of time to make things as easy on your mind as possible. Start being more direct when talking to others. Ask for help when you needed it rather than dropping hints. Delegate tasks with confidence. Clear communication is much easier on the mind than beating around the bush. It's a way to get things done as painlessly as possible.

Take some time to reflect on any things in your life that are complicated and think about some ways you might be able to simplify them. Taking the complexity out of daily life does worlds of good for the mind. You'll be a lot less stressed out when you pare things down to basics.

Dealing With The Stresses Of A Life Online

"Almost everything will work again if you unplug it for a few minutes...including you."
Anne Lamott

It is impossible to ignore the role that social media plays in all of our lives. The vast majority of people have online profiles on one or more websites. It has become the social norm to read, post, and share events from our lives online. There are of course varying degrees in which we each get involved with sites like these. Some of us use social media all day every day. Others use it when they are bored or when they have something special to share. A select few of us steer clear of it altogether. But it would be naive of me to write this book without mentioning life online, as it can be a very real source of stress in our lives. After all, online we're dealing with others on a forum with its own rules and boundaries, none of which are 100% clear. Interacting with people online can get complicated. In addition, the way we use social media can have direct effects on our self-esteem and our view of ourselves within the world around us.

Suffice to say, social networking plays a pretty substantial role in our stress levels. Most of us are contactable at all times these days which means less quiet time and an increased likeliness to work out-of-hours. Even our social lives have very little breathing room these days. We are expected to know everything our friends are up to if they've posted about it online. We are expected to share the things we like, to put a price, so to speak, on things that make us smile and frown. And when it comes to our working lives, social networking is more or less unavoidable. Whatever your career is, there's probably something about it online. If you're a business owner, your business probably has its own page. If you're an artist or musician, you will be expected to be constantly engaged with your fans. You will feel the pressure to be visible online. Work for a charity? You have to post about it online. Proud of your kid's performance in the school play? You better tell everyone you've ever known about it! It can be enjoyable at times, awful at others, but life online will almost inevitably cause you added stress at one point or another.

The thing about social networking is that you never know what you're going to get. One day everything seems light hearted and kind, and the next day it's negative and hateful. The pressure to keep up with life online is enough without the very likely possibility that you're going to see some things you wish you hadn't. Things that can make your mood take a nose dive. So it's important to be able to harvest the good and weed out the bad. **To seek the positive, and ignore the negative.** We have to be able to protect ourselves from the added stress life online can throw our way. We have to evaluate how we use social media, and decide if it's good for us or bad for us. Being able to do this for yourself means that not only will you be able to avoid added stress, but that you'll also be able to use your online life to *reduce* and *relieve* stress.

The following two lists offer you some insight as to what you should be looking at online and what you should be avoiding. The aim here is not to encourage you to close all of your online accounts and go live in a hut in the forest. It's here to help you shape the way you use your life online so that you can get the most out of it while protecting yourself from the not-so-savory stuff.

Positive Things To Take From Social Media

1 - Things that are funny.
Seek out things online that will make you laugh. Laughter is a great stress buster. Enjoyment of life should be at the top of your list of priorities. If it's not, why bother trudging through all the things you *have* to do? Why keeping pushing forward if you're not going to get any release or relief? Life online can give you plenty of giggles. There are a lot of people in the world using social media to share laughter and lightness, and this is the stuff you want to see. Just be careful not to flock towards things that are funny because they're mean. Laughter that is rooted in hate and negativity shouldn't be the aim here. So choose your poison wisely and keep it light.

2 - Things that feed your soul.
Life online can be wonderfully heartening at times. News stories or videos about people overcoming obstacles can help you stay positive

when times are tough. Positive affirmations are all over the Internet so why not tap into this resource when you need a little pick-me-up? We all need to have our souls fed, yet so many of us overlook this vital necessity when we're pinned under a mile long to do list! When we're stressed out, we can easily forget that there are still a lot of good people in the world doing good things. If we're feeling frustrated or low, we need a reminder of the good things in the world. The people that are working to help others, the people who are making positive change in the world, these are the people we need to see online in order to regain our sense of hopefulness. Remember that input is as important as output. You've got to replenish your system if you're always *giving*. You have to balance how much energy you're putting out into the world with how much you are taking in. Life must have balance in order to be fulfilling. Our minds need to be stimulated and we need to take time to feel good about the people we share the earth with.

3 - Times of celebration.
Life is so busy in this day and age that celebration often gets pushed to the back of the line. We used to use times of celebration to relax and have fun. Weddings, bar mitzvahs, religious holidays, and birthday parties used to matter so much more than they do today. And now that so much of our lives are online, it's easy to quickly scroll past posts about marriage and the births of new babies. But if we take the time to really feel happy for others - not just long enough to hit the Like button and move onto the next thing - we are breeding new positivity. Being happy for other people is a good thing. It keeps us from becoming jealous or bitter, and reminds us of the bigger picture. It helps our view of humanity. On top of all that, when you allow yourself to celebrate on someone else's behalf, your relationships with them will also benefit. Remember that putting positive energy into the world is like sewing seeds. You'll always yield a return of that positivity.

4 - Moments of togetherness and unity.
Unity is extremely important to the human psyche. We have a fundamental need to be part of groups in order to be our best selves. We need to be around other people to increase the quality of our lives and we need to feel as though we are being heard and respected

by others. When things are difficult from a global, political, or personal standpoint, social networking can offer a way for us to come together to make a change. It can highlight events, ideas, and a support network for everyone living through the same crisis. There is always greater strength in numbers and social media is a great place to build that strength. So too, life online might mean being able to support a family member or friend who needs a helping hand but who lives far away. Friends going through difficult times may be comforted by their online support network when times are tough. And when you need support, using social networking to get in touch with the right people is a valuable asset. Seek out moments of togetherness and unity in your online life. Flock to people who are likeminded and steer clear of those who are likely to oppose or criticize you.

Another way you can become unified with others is via fundraisers and awareness sites. Crowd funding and charity events offer a chance not only to raise funds for people in need, but also to show our support for the causes we care most about. Furthermore, there's a lot of positivity and warmth to be found when people come together for a good cause. Getting involved might just secure a warm fuzzy feeling when you need one.

5 - Sharing an interest with others.
Social networking can be a wonderful place to meet people like you! Whether you want to get to know some local parents with children the same age as yours, or you'd like to connect globally with people who share an interest in the same hobbies as you. Life online offers a world of events, ideas, shared media, and resources from across the globe. It can be a great way to meet new people or to maintain relationships with those you have things in common with. It is important for us to feel a sense of belonging in life. We need to function within groups and we can do that online.

Things To Avoid Online

1 - Seeking personal validation.
I cannot stress this enough. Almost all of us will use life online to get the personal validation we need at one point or another; either

consciously or subconsciously. But relying on social networking to make you feel good about yourself often backfires. We all know what it feels like to post something online and only get a few *likes*. It's disappointing. It can make us doubt ourselves and our intentions. It can hurt our feelings. On the flip side of that, when you post something witty or meaningful and it gets a lot of *likes*, your confidence can soar. The thing is, using social media in this way can lead to a very flimsy emotional existence. You're flying high one day and feel like the scum of the earth the next.

Now, I'm not suggesting that you delete your online profiles if you enjoy life online. However, in your mind you have to create a wall between your personal self-beliefs and what happens online. How many *likes* you get in a day should not be allowed to rule your mood or affect your self-esteem. Because if you let it get into your head - validation or a lack there of - it might hit you where it counts. Having your mood affected by a few clicks of a mouse could leave you in a funk. That might mean that you get less done in a day. It might mean that you become irritable or short tempered. It might just throw you off your game for a while. And the thing is, it's just not worth it. If you're proud of what you post online, don't let the amount of *likes* you get change that. If you're unsure of the things you've posted, forgive yourself and move on. Don't give life online the power to make or break you. Keep in mind that there are a plethora of reasons you might not get the *likes* you desire because there are countless elements working at the same time. For instance, your friends might be busy or your post mightn't come up in their feed at all. If you're dating someone and they don't like your post, you might let yourself get caught up in self-doubt or worry, but it's always possible that something else is at work. **And that's something you have to keep in mind about life online: it's not always all about you.** Remember to slow down your thoughts if you find yourself rattled by something that happens online. Be calm and confident about who you are.

2 - Judging other people.
Using social networking as a means to keep track of people you don't like is just mean spirited. Spending your time judging people about what they post online is nothing more than breeding negativity

and we all know that too much negativity leads to heightened stress levels and difficult relationships. This type of habit is one that simply has to go. It's a waste of time and it can bring out the worst in you. The only way we can fully feel free to live our lives the way we want to is to agree to live and let live. **To each, their own**. What other people do is up to them, whether you agree with it or not. If you believe that someone you truly care about is making some bad choices, it might be worth talking to them about that. But as a general rule of thumb, if you are not prepared to say something to someone's face, keep it to yourself. Resist the urge to criticize or gossip. Your time could be much better spent.

3 - Stalking.
In the last decade or so, the word *"stalking"* has taken on a whole new meaning. But despite the fact that you're not secretly following someone around, stalking online means pretty much the same thing: watching people without them knowing about it. A lot of people indulge in this dirty little habit. They stalk their exes or people they'd like to date. They stalk old friends or coworkers. The Internet has made it possible to know a lot more about people than we used to. We can see where they are, who they're associating with, and what they're getting up to. So much of our lives are publicly documented these days. For some people, looking into the lives of others can be extremely tempting. There's a natural curiosity there, an itch that wants to be scratched. But obsessing about the comings and goings of others is a waste of time and it could leave you in a pretty crappy mood.

Plus, stalking is just plain weird! Think about it. If you are a single person, would you ever walk around town peeking in the windows of people who are getting married and having babies? No. Would you drive around looking to see what your boyfriend's ex is up to? Would you peer into the conversations they have with their friends and family? No. And if you did, you'd probably see something you wish you hadn't and end up feeling low, envious, angry, or disheartened. It's only natural that feelings like that would affect your stress levels.

Furthermore, spending your time this way might be eating into time that you could be using more productively. We have to look at this type of habit as something which is unnatural and unproductive. If you really want to know something about someone, ask them! If you wouldn't feel comfortable talking to them face to face about something, you might just be better off not knowing. Remember, curiosity killed the cat. So think before you stalk. If stalking is likely to make you feel bad about yourself or someone you know, stop before you start.

4 - Feeding negative emotions.
It's wonderful when social networking offers us things to feel good about but there are many times when what we're actually confronted with are things that make us feel bad in one way or another. For instance, if you've had a rotten day, going online and reading about your competitor's success is only going to make you feel worse. Looking at the profile of someone you're jealous of is rarely a positive mission. Looking at your ex and their new partner online is never a good idea. Going online in order to oppose people or fight with them is a pointless endeavor.

But sometimes when we're stressed out, we're drawn to negativity. When we're feeling bad about ourselves, we're more likely to seek out things that make us feel worse than we are to look for solutions that will make us feel better. It's a strange but common human compulsion. You might think of it as emotional self-harm or kicking yourself when you're down. Stress is usually a negative state of being, therefore you're going to be more susceptible to being wound up by little things. You might find yourself getting angry, frustrated, or critical of things you wouldn't really be bothered by if you were in a state of calm. So make sure to take this into account when you use social media. If you have a tendency to get worked up over things online, try to avoid it when stress is high. There will always be negativity online. It is up to you to avoid it and focus on the positive.

5 - Bad news.
If you use social media as your main source for news and current events, or you just happen to see a lot of news in your feed, you may

have noticed that the vast majority of news is negative. There are a lot of bad things that happen in the world and this has been the case since the beginning of time. But depending on what type of people you're *"friends"* with online, you could be inundated with streams of negative and/or hateful news. Obviously, there is nothing wrong with keeping up to date with current events, but if you've noticed that your mood dips after being online, it might be that you are simply being exposed to too much bad news.

It is extremely unfortunate that there is so much hate and tragedy in life, and all of us should do everything we can to be good citizens of the world. But the more sadness and grief we are exposed to, the more drained and hopeless we may become. This is especially true for people who are already feeling down or those who are sensitive by nature. Sad stories that your friends post online could be subconsciously weighing you down. And if you're already stressed out, you could find yourself experiencing a lack of motivation, productivity, or even losing the ability to cope. You might feel that the state of the world is hopeless and depressing.

So, as a general rule, if a negative post in your feed was written by someone you haven't seen or spoken to since you were eleven years old, you're allowed to move on without reading it. Protecting yourself from negative news stories doesn't mean being ignorant or flippant. It just means imposing a cut off limit. If you drink alcohol, think of it like going to the bar. You want to have a few drinks, have a good time, and get home early enough to avoid a hangover tomorrow. If you stay too late and have too many drinks, the next day is probably going to be a write off. Bad news is similar. We've all got to take in enough to be informed and aware, but not so much that we're left feeling disheartened, complacent, or hopeless.

6 - Things that make you angry.
Do you have a friend online who regularly posts things that make your blood boil? If so, stop following them!

Do you have a family member who acts like a know-it-all but has the wrong idea about just about everything? Stop following them!

Someone who never stops bragging about their kids when you're struggling with an unruly teenager? Stop following them!

Someone who posts every single thing they eat day in and day out? If it's bothering you, stop following them!

There is no point whatsoever in exposing yourself to these things if you don't want to see them. The last thing any of us need is more things to be angry about. Anger is toxic and it spreads like wildfire. And this particular type of anger is even harder to cope with because there is very little we can do with it. It's hard to turn it into something productive. But what we can do is avoid it, and sometimes that's all there is for it. Remember that there are ways to limit what kinds of posts you see in your feed without unfriending people. You can "hide" posts of a certain nature or from certain people without them even knowing about it. You just have to click that button.

7 - Things that make you bitter or resentful.
Bitterness and resentment is ripe for the picking all over social media. A lot of people online post things that they are proud of or excited about. That's innocent enough, and it's certainly better than angry rants. However, sometimes when we're exposed to the good things in other people's lives, it reminds us of the things we don't have in ours. If you're single and childless, it's natural to feel emotionally activated when it seems like everyone in your peer group is getting married and having kids. If you've been desperately trying to climb the corporate ladder and someone you don't particularly care for gets the promotion you deserved, seeing them celebrating online is bound to eat away at you. If you taught someone everything they know and they surpass you, it's going to hurt.

We have to remember that just like anger, bitterness and resentment are toxic. Jealousy can rage, and it's not always easy to shift. So start by protecting yourself. Unfollow or "hide" people that make you feel bad about yourself. Get out of any online groups that are affecting you negatively. Take a break from the Internet completely when your stress levels are particularly high. Stay offline when you're not in a good mood. Always remember that what you're doing with your life is just as valid as what everyone else is doing. If you do feel resentment often, try using it as a platform to get even more out of life. Use it as a driving force to be a better person and get what you want for yourself. Don't use it as a stick to beat yourself or anyone else with.

8 - Things that make you feel embarrassed, ashamed, or not good enough.

If you're prone to looking at posts online that make you feel like less of a person, stop it. There is a lot of pressure to keep up with the Joneses in this world, and as soon as we give into that pressure, it starts to eat away at us. It is natural to feel defeated in life from time to time, and unfortunately, we have no choice but to take the good with the bad. But we don't need to kick ourselves when we're down. If you went on a date with someone and it didn't end up working out, don't let their new relationship make you feel ashamed. If you applied for a promotion and someone else won over you, it is natural to feel like you're not good enough. So why go online and expose yourself to their public joy? Why torture yourself with things that are going to make you feel bad about yourself? Life is too short for that type of nonsense. Protect yourself from things like this as much as you possibly can. We will all feel embarrassment enough in our lives without seeking out more of it.

9 - Getting into political arguments.

The world we live in is changing constantly, and in many ways this could easily be viewed as terrible, frightening, unfair, and disheartening. But fighting with people online isn't usually the way forward. It's a very fast and easy way to get your hands on some extra stress, but it's not likely to do much more than that. Think about it, how often have you actually changed someone's mind about something on social media? How many times have you seen people fighting on social media and actually reach a respectful conclusion? I'm guessing not very often.

I would never suggest that you don't get involved in politics; I think we all have to do everything we can for justice and a more positive future. However, engaging in negative, cyclical debates online is unlikely to do anything other than leave you feeling drained, angry, and even more stressed out. We are lucky that in this day and age, we are all allowed have an opinion and a forum on which to express it. But it is also important to remember that some of your friends and family members won't agree with you all of the time. Furthermore, it is possible that you could offend, upset, or make people uncomfortable if you don't present your arguments clearly.

Remember that when we type things, our intonation is completely up for interpretation, so even when you type something in good spirits, it could be read as being antagonistic. If you do engage with political debates online, check in with yourself regularly by asking yourself if the debate is productive. If it is productive and you feel good about it, stick with it. If it seems like it's going nowhere, duck out of it.

What To Do:
Think about how much time you spend online.

Do you scroll through news feeds every time you're bored or at a loose end?
Do you dip in and out of it every day?
How do you use social media and what do you get out of it?
Are there certain people or subjects that regularly put you in a bad mood?
Do you feel like you're losing valuable time because you spend too much time online?
Have you noticed any changes in the way you socialize with people in person as a result of being too comfortable online?
Do you experience social anxiety or awkwardness?

Life online can be great. It can be informative, fun, and interesting. But it can also cause stress, frustration, anger, and resentment. So it's important that we all monitor how much time we spend online and how we use it. For the next week, try writing down how you feel after every session you have on social media. You can journal if you like but you could also simply write a single word down, such as "indifferent", "annoyed", or "jovial". When the week is over, have a look through your words. Can you identify any themes? Add up how many times you've written down words that are positive, negative, and neutral. This should help you see how life online is affecting you so that you adjust your habits accordingly.

Finally, remember that life online should not be your only means of communication and socializing. We need to be around people in the physical. Life online is what it is, but it's not a substitute for real life social interaction.

Stress With Friends, Family & Romantic Partners

"Don't smother each other. No one can grow in the shade."
Leo Buscaglia

It should come as no great surprise that stress can have seriously damaging effects on our relationships with others. This doesn't just include relationships with partners and spouses, but also our relationships with friends, family members and coworkers. But when it comes to stress and relationships, it's a two-way street. Yes, stress can hurt your relationships, but relationships can also cause stress. Conflicts with others are among the most stressful things we experience in life. Difficulties with your boss, your mother-in-law, your siblings, friends, or your partner at home are not easy to cope with.

Being able to resolve and recover from conflicts with others is a skill that we all need in order to protect ourselves from added stress. We need to be able to view situations realistically and honestly, rather than allowing our emotions to overtake us. Conflicts and confrontations are not easy, and reacting emotionally to them rarely leads us to a resolution. We need to be able to think clearly and rationally, and we need to be able to view the situation from all angles. This means not focusing entirely on yourself, but also taking into account what the person you're dealing with is thinking and feeling as well. Of course, it's not always easy to stay cool, calm, and collected, but with effort any one of us can learn to slow things down, retrain our thinking, and learn to better manage relationship difficulties.

It is only natural for human beings to be self-focused. After all, our own feelings, perceptions and experiences are the only things we can be certain of when dealing with other people. However, if we practice seeing things from different points of view, our relationships will benefit in leaps and bounds. When conflicts occur, you have to be curious about what's going on outside of yourself.

Is the person you're dealing with confused, hurt, or disappointed?

Are they acting out of fear or insecurity?
Has there been a miscommunication?
Are they lashing out at you because something else is going on with them?
What would it feel like to be them right now?

Thinking like this is extremely important when it comes to successful communication and conflict resolution. We have to stop being defensive and start being curious as to what lies beneath the conflict for both parties. Furthermore, we have to ask ourselves why we're reacting the way we are.

Did someone say something in particular that triggered you?
Is that because they meant to hurt you or did they accidentally hit a weak spot?
Why are you feeling the way you're feeling?
Are either one of you potentially overreacting?
Are other things in life affecting your relationships?

I cannot stress enough the importance of regular self-reflection in circumstances like these. The more we question our own feelings and actions, the better we will understand our reactions to external forces. The more we try to gain perspective and open ourselves up to other people's way of thinking, the easier it will be to overcome conflict.

Unfortunately, not all conflicts can be resolved easily, and some may never be resolved. Sometimes the best way to deal with difficult situations like this is to try to reach to a point of respectful disagreement. If you can't see a way out of a conflict, it might be better to just let it go and move on. There's only so long you can let something eat away at you. After a while, you might need to ask yourself how important the issue really is. Is it worth driving yourself crazy over? If it's something you can't let go of, try to take a little break from it and reassess the situation a few days later. You might need some time to process your feelings if someone was hurtful towards you. Emotional wounds take time to heal, whether you're feeling sad, rejected, or angry. A little bit of distance might be good for you if you can get it. At the end of the day, a good way to think about conflict resolution is by asking yourself if you want to win the fight or if you'd rather end the fight. It's not always easy to let go when you know you're right about something but if the conflict isn't going anywhere productive, everyone might be better off by just ending it. Agree to disagree and move on with your life.

As I mentioned briefly earlier in this book, one thing you may want to consider is putting up some boundaries in your relationships with others. We all have at least one friend or family member who can be insensitive or outright hurtful towards us. And for some reason, many of us continue to back this person again and again with things that are close to our heart, only to end up feeling hurt or dismayed by their response. Remember that you don't have to tell anyone *everything* that's going on in your life. We all deserve and require privacy. With people who are insensitive or rude, you might be better off talking to them about less important things. Why talk to them about things that are close to your heart if they're only going to make you regret telling them? If a subject comes up which is likely to set either of you off, you're allowed to say that you'd rather talk about something else. You need to have boundaries in place in order to protect yourself.

Furthermore, if you have people in your life who are draining or who put an unreasonable amount of pressure on you, you've got to put a boundary in place. Limit the amount of time you're willing to spend with them. Get plenty of time with people who make you feel good about yourself and the world around you. If you're feeling a bit low on energy or mood, don't hang out with someone who is likely to drag you further down. You don't have to end your relationship with them. Just plan to see them when you're strong enough to bear their weight.

Boundaries are an extremely important facet of our relationships with others. When we have them properly in place, our relationships are less likely to become stressful. If your mother-in-law regularly crosses the line with your kids, put a boundary in place. Make it clear and firm without being hurtful. If you have a friend who picks on you a lot, put a boundary in place. Tell them how you feel about their behavior and be clear about which subjects you'd like them to avoid. If you have a sibling that regularly questions or judges your choices, put a boundary in place. Don't talk to them about those particular choices or tell them that you're not looking for advice on the subject. You get the drift. Without boundaries, relationships can go sour pretty quickly. We can't constantly step on each other's toes and expect things to stay peachy all the time.

Most importantly, we need to protect ourselves from conflicts that are *avoidable*. Boundaries prevent conflict. They put order and rules into our relationships. They make it easier to express our feelings and keep our relationships focused on positive things. They are a way to protect ourselves from conflict and confrontation. Maintaining relationships isn't easy. It takes work and thoughtfulness. But, when dealt with properly, our relationships with others can be the most comforting, exciting, and motivating things in our lives.

Difficulties in romantic relationships have added layers of complexity. Stress can take a huge toll on relationships between partners and spouses. These are the people that are closest to you. They are the people who see your ugly moments, the ones who often bear the brunt of your stress. When stress is high in a household, it can be pretty tough to get perspective and turn things around, but there are ways to achieve household serenity. Start by keeping complaining to a minimum. It is wonderful to have someone you can share your inner most feelings with, but we all have to be careful that we don't drain the people who are closest to us. Relationships need balance. They need some good to weigh out the bad. They need some gratitude and affection to balance out the difficulties of daily life. We need to appreciate one another and remember to keep having fun together. Focusing on positive things together makes you twice as strong. Dwelling on negative things or complaining about other people together, makes you twice as weak.

How often do you think about how you greet your partner after a long day at work? How do you wind down at night? Intimate relationships should be a space for emotional safety and support. They should be a place where you can push the reset button when you're frustrated with other parts of life. But often, this isn't the case.

The longer we're with someone, the more likely we are to let things become negative. We're more likely to complain and whine about all the things that are bothering us. We're likely to take our anger out on each other and take each other for granted. But there are things we can do to prevent that from happening and to get things back on track if they've gone a bit sour. The way we greet one another is a great place to start. When you come home from work, before you say a single word, give your partner a ten second kiss. Leave your baggage at the door. Look at your partner, and hold them. Then take a deep breath and remember that you're in your safe space now. After your kiss, get into the habit of each saying three positive things that happened that day before launching into anything else. No matter how rubbish your day was, force yourself to identify three good things that happened. If nothing spectacular happened to you, maybe you just had a great sandwich for lunch! Maybe you got a nice text from a friend. It doesn't matter what it is but taking the time to do this is a fantastic way to fix your mindset for the rest of the evening.

You can also do this in the morning before work. Each of you say three things that you love about each other, or your kids, your past, or your life in general. This may sound like a frivolous practice but I promise you, it can have dramatic effects on your general outlook on life. It's a calming and encouraging practice that can keep the unity you have with your partner on positive terms. This is a way to create balance in your relationship. Most couples share their stress to some degree. By doing this, you are also sharing your positivity, joy, and hope for the future.

Lastly, it's important for me to note that it would be naive to assume that all conflicts can be resolved. Sometimes a relationship has gone too far down the negative route. Sometimes your stress about work colleagues outweighs the things you like about your job. Sometimes you'll need to re-evaluate your friendships. These are not easy things to cope with. They are not decisions that are easily made. But, if you feel like you need to make a big life change and you have considered all your options with a clear mind, you might just need to get it done.

Maybe you'll need to end a relationship, start a new one, get some space, take a leap, or do something risky. Times of change and challenge aren't the easiest things to cope with, but life is too short to spend it being miserable.

Endings are one of the hardest things we have to cope with in life. Whether we're talking about getting a divorce, quitting a job, or saying goodbye to a friend who's moving far away, it's going to be difficult. But eventually you will heal, and you will live past it. As long as you are doing what's right in your heart, you should be able to move forward in life without any regrets.

Leave Stress Behind. Live A Happier Life.

"Very little is needed to make a happy life; it is all within yourself, in your way of thinking."
Marcus Aurelius

This is your life. You're only going to get one chance to live it. We don't get to go back in time and redo any of this. So you have to ask yourself in all honestly, how you want to feel in later life?

Do you want to look back and regret how much time you spent being stressed out?
Do you want to feel as though you wasted time focusing too much on the negative parts of life?
Do you want to regret losing relationships because you were unable to cope with stress?

Or do you want to look back and feel like you had the life you wanted?
Do you want to look back and feel proud of yourself for getting through your stressful moments?

When it comes to stress, we've got to get perspective on things. We need to have fun and enjoy our lives. Yes, we need to get things done and we need to make money. Those are unavoidable parts of life. But they don't mean that we have to be *all* work and *no* play. They don't mean that we can't take care of ourselves in the meantime. They don't mean that we have to miss our children growing up or that we waste our youthful vibrance trying to be more serious adults. Sure, life is serious. But it's also fun, exciting, fulfilling, and free.

For each of us, stress will come and go. We will go through tough times. We will have a hard time seeing the good parts of life when we're consumed by all the unavoidable mundanities. But it doesn't have to be like that all the time. There are things we can do to lessen the stress we feel and get greater enjoyment and peace from our lives.

Getting structure in our lives works.
Keeping our bodies healthy works.
Taking time to reflect on our feelings and experiences works.
Taking time to have fun works.
Being excited about personal growth works.
Maintaining boundaries in our relationships works.

You are full of answers to stress's most prominent problems **now**. All there is to do now is to be committed to giving yourself the life you desire. Go easy on yourself. Be kind to yourself. And remember, try not to take yourself too seriously. This moment should be a turning point for you. What are you going to do with it?

"The past cannot be changed. The future is still in your power"
Unknown Author

If You Have Time, Could You Do Me A Favor?

Thank you so much for checking out my book.

I sincerely hope you got value from it. I hope it allows you to make important changes in your life. I hope this book helps you decrease your stress and increase your happiness.

If you liked this book could you possibly taking 60 seconds to write a quick blurb about this book on Amazon?

Reviews are a vital way for books to get more exposure and help to spread the message. Mental health is not a small issue. We need people to talk about it. Stress and other conditions should not be ignored or hidden.

If you have time and you are willing, I would appreciate if you could leave a review by going to the books page on Amazon.

Thank you. Your support is very much appreciated.

Printed in Great Britain
by Amazon